FORGOTTEN
FACTORS

FORGOTTEN
FACTORS

ROY
HESSION

CHRISTIAN ❖ LITERATURE ❖ CRUSADE
Fort Washington, Pennsylvania 19034

CHRISTIAN LITERATURE CRUSADE

U.S.A.
P.O. Box 1449, Fort Washington, PA 19034

GREAT BRITAIN
51 The Dean, Alresford, Hants., SO24 9BJ

AUSTRALIA
P.O. Box 419M, Manunda QLD 4879

NEW ZEALAND
10 MacArthur Street, Feilding

Copyright © 1976
Christian Literature Crusade
London
This Printing 1998

ISBN 0-87508-234-3

Scripture quotations are generally from the *Authorized Version (K.J.V.)* of the Bible with the occasional substitution of words commonly accepted as giving the sense more accurately to today's reader. A few quotations are from the *Revised Standard Version of the Bible,* copyrighted ©1946, 1952, 1971, 1973, and used by permission, and from the *English Revised Version* of 1881; the former is referred to in the footnotes as R.S.V. and the latter as R.V.

PRINTED IN THE UNITED STATES OF AMERICA

CONTENTS

5

FOREWORD

The subtitle of this book — An Aid to Deeper
Repentance — must be taken seriously if my dear friend
Roy Hession's purpose in writing it is to be fulfilled. After
fifteen or twenty years of softening-up by worldly
influences in the Church, including the statement in court
by an Anglican bishop that the adultery in a certain novel
was a form of "holy communion," we are not likely to find
this call to deeper repentance in this area of life
comfortable.

The worship of Eros has become as much a feature of the
western world as was its parallel cult at Ephesus in the days
of St. Paul. God's standards are the same now as then; but
as this book stresses, His grace is the same too.

Chapter 7 says "The church at Corinth was a church of
converted and delivered fornicators, adulterers, homosexuals, thieves, and drunkards. And why not? — that is
what the church is meant to be, a bunch of sinners, saved
by the grace of God!"

This is how the grace of God is magnified by the author,
and as he takes us deeper into the nature of sin we find that

7

none of us is guiltless and so all of us are candidates for the grace of God which comes to us through the death and resurrection of the Lord Jesus Christ.

If the book achieves its purpose of moving us to deeper repentance it will also enable us to know and enjoy the grace of God in a new and deeper way.

EDDY STRIDE

Rector of Christ Church,
Spitalfields, London
England

1

STRANGE TITLE?

No sins cause so much sorrow and shame and so many unhappy complications, both personal and social, as sins of sex. In traveling during the past forty years all over the British Isles, the United States, and other parts of the world ministering the gospel of Christ, I have found myself brought into contact with many situations of great need, sorrow, and perplexity which have been brought about by what I have called in the subtitle of this book "sexual misbehavior." I have found these situations abounding on all hands, sometimes within the church itself, either among its new converts who have yet to be disentangled from some aspects of their former life or among its older members who have been taken captive.

The purpose of this first chapter is to outline the meaning and scope of this little book with its apparently strange subtitle set out in full on the title page: "An Aid to Deeper Repentance of the Forgotten Factors of Sexual Misbehavior." Even while we survey the problems and miseries caused by man's sin, we know (or ought to know) that the grace of God has a complete answer to all such problems. God's grace is ever greater than man's sin. As someone has said, "Jesus delights not only to forgive the messer, but to unmess the mess." Once things go wrong in a life, His only concern is with recovery. He does not hold inquests or seek to apportion blame, but simply asks each in turn the question He asked the paralytic at the pool of Bethesda long ago, "Wilt thou be made whole?" For it is in the area of recovering the losses, complications, and miseries caused by man's sin that He is expert. If I may say so, He is at His best here and it is His innumerable successes in the realm of recovery that make His name great.

But (and this is an important but) the answer of God's undeserved grace is ever contingent on man's unreserved repentance. Only in the place of repentance do men become candidates for the grace of God. Today, however, repentance has become the missing note of the gospel. Men do not know how to repent. Even among Christians the call to repent falls strangely on their ears, especially when it is addressed to *them,* and not only to those that are without. More than that, men do not know where to repent, in particular with regard to sexual misbehavior and the situations created by it. So often they do not see the basic wrong they have committed. If they repent at all, it might almost be said they are repenting of the wrong things. The factors in such misbehavior with which a moral God must be inevitably most concerned have been forgotten, and because there has not been repentance *there*, in the matter about which God has been most contending with them, the full answer of His grace is not experienced and the wonderful recovery He would have given them is never fully theirs.

It is to highlight these forgotten factors that these pages

are written, in the hope that some may be able, under the conviction of the Holy Spirit, to humble themselves and repent of those basic wrongs which they have committed, and that in thus repenting they may taste the sweetness of the grace of God for sinners, a grace that not only forgives the sinner but makes over again the marred vessel — himself and his situation — so that he may have boundless cause to sing:

> "Who is a pardoning God like Thee,
> Or who has grace so rich and free?"

If the purpose of the book is to be "an aid to deeper repentance," as the subtitle suggests, it is only that it may offer help and encouragement to the sinner — what the Apostle Paul calls "everlasting consolation and good hope through grace."[1]

I realize that when it comes to matters of sexual behavior, nearly everybody regards himself as an expert! There has been so much airing of the subject these years, that many have well-developed ideas on the subject and for that reason some may be inclined to read these chapters rather quizzically. But they have been written to those in desperate need, as a sort of life-line cast out to them as they struggle with the waves. If it be thought that the approach to these problems is somewhat simplistic and does not take account of modern thought on the subject, I like to think it is because the Bible itself is simplistic, calling sin, sin, without apology, but offering to every penitent the plenteous grace of God that covers all his failures and redeems him out of all his troubles.

These chapters are not concerned with merely giving

---

1. 2 Thess. 2:16.

good advice and suggesting guidelines for human behavior to prevent wrongs being committed and grave damage being done. They assume rather that the wrong has already been committed, that the damage has already been done, that it is now too late for good advice. The question now is, Is there any good news to give to people in such a condition? The answer is yes, a thousand times yes.

2

FORGOTTEN FACTORS

Today our society is so sex-obsessed that if it thinks of wrong sexual behavior at all, it seems to think of it only in terms of the illicit sex act itself — the lustfulness of it, the uncleanness of it, the uncontrolled passion of it, the perverted use of it. If that is the main wrong of sexual misbehavior, it is easy for men to make excuses for themselves and to side-step the conviction of the Holy Spirit. "Surely," they say, "it is something merely biological, something quite natural. It is purely arbitrary on the part of society, even of God, to draw a line and say that before a certain date-line the act is wrong, but after that date-line it is right. What is done may be lustful, but it is none the less natural." If the main sinfulness of such misbehavior is the lustfulness and impurity of the act itself, it is easy for men to argue in this way.

Strange to say, that is the aspect with which the Bible, which is the only expression of the mind of God we have on the subject, is least concerned. Make no mistake, the Bible does condemn unequivocally sexual misbehavior because of its lustfulness and uncleanness. The fact that our

Authorized Version describes such sins in Elizabethan English has robbed its words of much of their meaning for the modern mind. Fornication, adultery, effeminate, abusers of themselves with mankind, uncleanness, lasciviousness, inordinate affection, evil concupiscence are the words used. But what do they mean to the modern English-speaking man? Once we exchange those words for their present-day equivalents — promiscuity, immorality, unfaithfulness, prostitution, homosexuality, masturbation, lesbianism, lustful imaginations, indulgence in pornographic literature, etc. — we all know what the Bible is talking about. And it is surprising how much it does speak about these things. There is not one of Paul's epistles, addressed, mark you, to Christians, in which he does not speak about them and the people who do them. And when we hear him say, "for which things' sake the wrath of God cometh on the children of disobedience,"[1] and again, "of the which I tell you before, as I have told you in time past, that they which do such things shall not inherit the kingdom of God,"[2] there is no doubt at all that the Bible condemns these things for their lustfulness, impurity, and perversion.

But even so, I say again, that is the aspect with which the Bible seems to be less concerned. It speaks about the physical aspects of sex, both right and wrong, with a complete absence of squeemishness or shock. Though nothing is hidden in its accounts, it is very difficult for even the most lustful of readers to get a vicarious enjoyment out of the things alluded to — mainly because that is not the purpose for which it is written, which certainly cannot be said of many of the books that are published today, even when they purport to be great literature. All the allusions

1. Col. 3:6.   2. Gal. 5:21.

in Scripture to sex, even to the most degraded forms of sex, are clean; and more, they are penetrating. God is out to get to the bigger wrongs behind these things, where men are utterly culpable and without excuse, where the offence is seen to be against eternal moral principles, which are part of God's own nature and are written into man's nature in his conscience. And here, of course, we are in the realm where sexual misbehavior is no different from any other misbehavior. Sin is simple self-centeredness, independence of God, and that is basically always the same. It is only the raw material in which sin operates which changes. One man's raw material may be sexual desire; another's may be a desire for the top. It is the degree in which a man indulges himself in his particular raw material in defiance of the known will of God that constitutes the degree of his sinfulness. God then insists on judging sexual misbehavior on the same principles as He judges any other misbehavior, and that, rightly understood, is what makes His judgment such an awesome thing for us.

The factors, however, which constitute the real wrong of sexual misbehavior have been largely forgotten today. When men and women in some crisis of their lives try to repent of their sins along this line, they seldom get beyond confessing the lustfulness and impurity of them. God, however, wants to get to something deeper than that, in which they are far more culpable — such things as the wrong which one person inflicts on another through sexual misbehavior, the multiplied duplicities which are invariably involved in such misadventures, the dishonor a person does to his own body through abuse of its powers, and above all, the wrongs done to a loving God. These are some of the forgotten factors which one so seldom hears confessed. Those who might assert they have repented might find on closer examination that they have never really faced the more culpable aspects of their deeds, and for that reason have not ever really experienced the full answer of the grace of God. Sometimes a man who has come to Christ and accepted Him as his Saviour is obviously lacking in his experience of the grace of God. His testimony is somehow not a sinner's testimony, and he does not seem to possess a sinner's joy in his all-forgiving Saviour. It may be there has not been repentance at the level that God wants it. It may be he has not seen the most culpable factors in his sin, or if he has seen them, he has conveniently forgotten them.

So we come to consider in detail the forgotten factors in the various forms of sexual misbehavior — and indeed in all misbehavior.

3

THE FORGOTTEN FACTOR IN ADULTERY

Nowhere are the basic factors in sexual misbehavior so clearly revealed, for those who are willing to see them, as in the Bible record of King David's misbehavior in the matter of Bathsheba, the wife of one of his soldiers. What makes it so instructive for us is that it is not merely an account of a man's sordid deed, but of God acting with regard to it, showing Himself to be a God of truth and judgment on the one hand, but of mercy and grace on the other. It is the story, not only of the failure of an otherwise great and godly king, but of how God gloriously and fully recovered that failure. It has become famous in the world merely because of the sordidness which it expresses; but that is not the reason it is recorded in the Bible. It is recorded to reveal God's glory in restoring a sinner like David, in recovering even the situation that he created for himself, and in using all the disciplines and chastisements involved to further him in the path of sainthood and fellowship with Himself. So in spite of the unhealthy interest the world might show in the story, it is the preacher of the gospel who has the first right to it. Indeed, he is the only one who truly understands it.

Let us recount briefly the first part of the story. While his army was away on maneuvers against various enemies, David was at Jerusalem. He rose from his afternoon rest one day to walk in the cool of the evening on the roof of his house, from which he saw a beautiful woman washing herself in what she thought was the privacy of her garden. David's passions were aroused toward her, and he went indoors to inquire as to who she was. He learned that the woman living in that house was the wife of one of his soldiers away at that time in the fighting. He had her visit him and on that first occasion misconduct took place. She returned to her home to resume her normal life, without anyone knowing what had taken place, the whole matter being a secret between the two of them. Much else follows, but let us stop there for the moment.

There is nothing unusual in this story thus far. Alas, this sort of thing happens again and again in human life, and the record would hold little interest, except for the pornographically-minded, were it not that in this case God is seen acting with regard to what has been done. Contrary to what many people think, the only thing that makes human life really interesting is God acting with regard to it. What is happening today has been happening all down the centuries; man is never so unoriginal as in his sins. But once we hear of God acting with regard to a life and its failures, the story tingles with interest, for a new and ever fresh factor has entered. There is no meeting that tingles with more interest than a meeting for personal testimony; if the reader has never sat in one he has missed one of the most absorbing of the church's activities. But of what interest is it to us to hear a person merely tell of the sort of life he has been living, the dissatisfaction of it, the failures with which it has been marked? If that were all, it would be a dreary recital, which could be matched many times over from our own and others' experience. But when the person goes on to tell of how God has acted with regard to it, and that He has done so in grace rather than judgment, and that with the happiest results, every word is followed with keenest interest, and at the end the listeners can scarce refrain from giving audible praise to God. It takes God acting and moving to make life thrilling and absorbing!

So it is with this record before us, which we have for the moment cut short at this point. Nobody knew what David had done, but of course God did, and He is going to move with regard to it. His first movement must of necessity be conviction, the revelation of the true sinfulness of the act. For a time no word comes from heaven. David is left with his sin upon his conscience. He tells us in one of his psalms what he went through during that time: "When I kept silence, my bones waxed old through my groaning all the day long. For day and night thy hand was heavy upon me; my moisture is turned into the drought of summer."[1] Even so it is doubtful if he had any conception of the true sinfulness of what he had done. At last God sends to him Nathan the prophet to convey His message. In that message nothing is said about the lustfulness, the impurity, the uncontrolled passion expressed in his deed. A simple story is told of a callous wrong which one man has inflicted on another, and Nathan tells the story as if he was requiring the king's legal judgment on the matter. He told of a certain rich farmer possessed of great herds of cattle and flocks and sheep. Not far from him there lived a poor cottager, whose only capital, if such it could be called, was one ewe lamb. Maybe he intended to breed from her, but meantime it had become the household pet, the darling of

1. Ps. 32:3-4.

the children. A traveler comes unexpectedly to stay with the wealthy man. In order to provide for his entertainment the rich man spares ''to take of his own flock and of his own herd [of which he had so many], . . . but took the poor man's lamb, and dressed it for the man who was come to him.''[2] Nothing can match the simple drama of the words of our Authorized Version at this point. ''And David's anger was greatly kindled against the man; and he said to Nathan, As the Lord liveth, the man who hath done this thing shall surely die; and he shall restore the lamb fourfold, because he did this thing, and because he had no pity. And Nathan said to David, Thou art the man.''[3]

Till that moment David had never seen what he had really done. In taking the wife of one of his soldiers in the ranks, he had done precisely what the rich man had done — an act which had so aroused his anger. He who had no lack of wives and concubines, according to the royal custom of those days, must needs seduce the one wife of one of his common soldiers, and that behind his back when he was serving the king in the field, thus breaking up his home and ruining his happiness. Even if her act was never found out, even if it was never repeated, it was quite certain that she would never feel the same toward her husband. And who knows for what further excursions into forbidden things it might have given her a taste? The thing that God was convicting David of was not the lustfulness and impurity of what he had done, but the callous wrong he had inflicted on another man. This had been to David one of the forgotten factors in his sexual misbehavior.

This is the aspect of the matter that God wants to show us and of which we must deeply repent if we are to know peace with Him — the grievous wrong we have done to

2. 2 Sam. 12:4.   3. 2 Sam. 12:5-7.

another. It is significant that the command, "Thou shalt not commit adultery,"[4] is not grouped with those of the ten commandments on the first table of stone, those that relate to our responsibilities toward God, but it is among those on the second table of stone, those that relate to our relationship toward our fellows. The commands on the first table are summarized in Christ's words, "Thou shalt love the Lord thy God with all thy heart,"[5] while those on the second by the words, "Thou shalt love thy neighbour as thyself."[6] Adultery is therefore a transgression of the law of love for one's neighbor. Someone might argue that his adultery is because of love, love for the woman, and that therefore it is no infringement of the law of love. Whatever it may be toward the woman, it is certainly not love toward her husband. Adultery represents the most callous transgression of another person's rights, interests, and feelings that is possible, and very often the circumstances in which it is committed and practiced (for it is usually not an isolated act, but a procession of them) make such behavior many times more detestable and culpable. Not only is the fact that the command "Thou shalt not commit adultery"[7] appears on the second table significant, but the position in which it appears there is even more significant. It comes in between "Thou shalt do no murder" and "Thou shalt not steal," and God regards it in the same category. It is in a very real sense stealing — stealing another person's husband or wife, stealing another's most intimate happiness, breaking up another person's home.

Strange as it may seem, God appears to take a most active interest in this side of life, and in a special way He feels Himself involved in this violation of another man's

4. Ex. 20:14.
6. Matt. 22:39.
5. Matt. 22:37.
7. Matt. 19:18 (R.V.).

rights. Indeed He distinctly declares Himself the avenger of all such. In Thessalonians Paul says, " . . . that no man transgress and wrong his brother in the matter"[8] (and the context makes it quite clear that the matter referred to is that of sexual relations), *"because that the Lord is the avenger of all such."* And again in Hebrews we read, "Let marriage be had in honour among all, and let the bed be undefiled, *for fornicators and adulterers God will judge."*[9]

When a person has attained his desires and what looks like a new happiness in a new marriage, it is easy to forget the price that has had to be paid for it, not paid by him but by somebody else. Somebody else has paid the price of losing his life-companion; somebody else has shed tears far into the night; somebody else has been robbed of his happiness; somebody else has had his home broken up; somebody else has been left lonely, struggling along on his own; children have been left without a father, or a mother. It is easy to forget the terrible wrongs another has suffered as we enjoy our new love. But God does not forget. Over the years He continues to say what He said to Cain, "The voice of thy brother's [or sister's] blood crieth unto me from the ground."[10] And such will never know peace with Him until he repents deeply of these grievous wrongs done to another. The time will come for such, as it comes in every life, when he or she will need God desperately and all the help He can give, but will not find Him while these wrongs remain unrepented of and therefore unforgiven by Him.

Of course, all such situations are bedeviled by convenient rationalizations which blind each participant to his real wrongs in the case. It is so often said that he or she

8. 1 Thess. 4:6 (R.V.).　　9. Heb. 13:4 (R.V.).　　10. Gen. 4:11.

was never really happy with his partner; they had a dog's life; life was unbearable. How easy it is for such factors to be grossly exaggerated in order to justify what was done! And even where such things are true (and of course such unhappiness is all too frequent), they were content to bear it and "make a go of it," and to do so indefinitely — until another party came on the scene for whom there was a special attraction. And no wrong need have been done had not that party consented. In many cases the real reason for the breakup of a home was not the impossibility of the first partner but the desirability of the second. But even where there is ungainsayable unhappiness in a partnership, there is no justification for a third party to steal one who is another's. A man may neglect his car, may never clean it, and allow it to get into a run-down condition, but that is no ground for another to appropriate it because he thinks he can look after it better. If we still try to justify adultery, the acid test is to ask ourselves, does the other husband or wife feel we have done him a service in relieving him of his partner and enjoying the attractions of that one? In spite of the fact that that partnership might not have been a happy one, when such a thing happens the other husband or wife always feels incensed against the one who has done it, because his rights have been infringed. In many cases it is much more — a whole welter of bitterness and unhappiness is set up.

I think that women especially need to be helped to see their wrong in the light of what they have done to the other woman. Very often a "mushy" sentiment is added to all the usual rationalizations and makes them blind to the facts as God sees them. Very often the pity motive becomes strong in a woman as she hears the story of unhappiness which the man tells her. She begins to feel that she can give the man what his wife does not give him. She might even persuade herself that it is a noble act for which she must be willing to brave even the censure of her own family. More often there is pride in it, in the feeling that she is succeeding in satisfying a man where his wife has failed. All of this makes her lose sight of the factor that God ever looks upon, the grievous wrong done to the other woman. Even when such a transgressor comes to receive Jesus Christ as her Saviour, it is doubtful sometimes how far she has repented of her part in this matter and therefore how far she knows the full healing and restoration of the grace of God.

I know of a situation where a man fell for the attractions of another woman and became unfaithful to his wife. His wife divorced him and he married the other woman. Now years later they have all three been converted to God and received Jesus Christ as their Saviour. The man is uneasy about the situation, but his second wife is quite content for things to remain as they are and sees no reason for concern. I do not know the situation intimately, but I cannot help wondering if the second wife ever stops to think that another woman is living alone in lodgings, going out to work to support herself, doing without the companionship once precious to her — all because she stole the husband and thereby broke up that home. Doubtless she confesses the wrong of the lustfulness of her first association with the man and acknowledges they were not right to have let themselves go; but that is the least important factor in the situation. One wonders if she has ever humbled herself before God to confess the wrong she has done to that other woman as sin against God, whether she has ever been to that other woman to confess it and crave her forgiveness and ask what can be done to put it right.

When an incident like this is described in this way, we immediately start asking what we think are very practical questions, especially if we are involved in such situations. What am I supposed to do to put it right? Have I got to give up the one I am living with — and what about the children? Or in another situation it may be asked, must I tell my husband, my wife, about what has happened? Is it not better to leave the present partner in ignorance? Very often these questions are being asked before there has been true repentance, before this thing has been deeply judged before God as sin. God would say to us, ''Do *that* first, and you will be assured of My forgiveness. After that I will show you what I want you to do with regard to putting things right with another, and when you are to do it.'' The essential thing is to repent truly and confess it to God; the situation then is in His hands, hands that can make all things new. We must therefore let Him guide us as to what He wants us to do in the matter of restitution — and He will not always want us to rush here. Sometimes to seek the counsel of another experienced Christian who will be faithful to us is helpful in ascertaining the will of God.

4

THE FORGOTTEN FACTOR
IN FORNICATION

In this chapter I have to use the old English word "fornication," because there does not seem to be a modern equivalent; not that the thing described is not prevalent, but because, I imagine, today we do not like to face things squarely and call them by the ugly name they deserve.

The difference between adultery and fornication is simply that adultery is sexual misbehavior in a case where one or both of the parties are married to another, whereas fornication is sexual misbehavior between parties neither of whom is married. Adultery is regarded by the law as violating the legal contract of marriage, whereas in the case of fornication there is no legal contract to violate. For that reason people have come to regard this act more lightly than adultery. Indeed, it might be argued that the element of wrong done to another, about which we have been speaking, is not present in fornication as in adultery. There is no doubt that it is the popular view that here one is not doing any harm to any third party, and therefore it does not matter, and so this thing is largely unrepented of.

Here especially, if we think only of the lustfulness of the

act itself, we shall find it easy to argue that after all it is natural and biological, and that today the older codes of morals have changed. But again it is the grievous wrong done to another that God wants to uncover, and in spite of the popular view, He sees it to be as much wrong here as in adultery, and certainly the fornicator will have to repent every bit as much as the adulterer if he is to know peace with God.

There is the wrong done to another, first of all, in that a man or woman has provoked another to do that which is against his conscience. In spite of all the modern ''advanced'' ideas on the subject, in spite of all the current psychological rationalizations on the subject, people still feel this to be wrong. All the radical talk and writings have signally failed to take away man's guilty conscience about fornication. And when a man seduces a girl, or when a lustful woman provokes a young man, he or she is inciting the other to do something that will be a stain on his honor, a festering sore on his conscience, something more for him to hide and tell lies about. That in turn may bring him into a condition which one day will lead him to a psychiatrist's consulting room seeking treatment for his tormented mind. Is that not inflicting a grievous wrong upon one's fellow? A man's or a woman's honor and good conscience are his most precious possession, the foundation of his mental and psychological well-being. How guilty then is the person who callously helps to rob him of it!

Then there is the grievous wrong done to another in that the man or woman may be starting the other on the slippery slope of further illicit sexual indulgence and promiscuity. Who knows but that the girl or young man led on by the other may be given a taste for something that will not stop there, that a fire will be kindled that will mean the moral degradation of that one in promiscuity and worse. In the eyes of God the moral responsibility is laid at the door of the one who started him off on that slope, or who helped him on after he had begun. Make no mistake about it, sex even in the best and purest is a smoldering fire, and to play with it is like pouring kerosine on a fire. We must not excuse ourselves with the thought that the one we have been involved with has never since gone very far down that slope. We have none the less been responsible for pushing that one just so far along it and making it just so much the more possible for him to go further. In attempting to avoid responsibility along this line, some men will proudly say they have never touched a virgin, that all those with whom they have had relations had fallen before. They do not escape responsibility before God. They must bear their share of the blame of producing the moral dereliction of that person. Whereas somebody must bear the blame for starting her off so that she became ''fair game'' for this later man, he must accept the responsibility of adding to her shame. The man who wants the peace and restoration that Jesus Christ gives will have to repent of all his fornications as having inflicted grievous wounds on those with whom he has been involved; and God may even send him to seek this or that one out to ask forgiveness for the wrong done.

Sometimes fornication inflicts upon an unmarried girl the cruel wrong of bearing a child outside of wedlock. Who can assess the shame and sorrow and life-long liability of such a thing both to the girl and her parents? And yet the man may go on his way careless and unconcerned only to do the same thing to yet another girl. Some years ago I read a long article featured in an American magazine on ''The Unmarried Mother.'' Much of the article consisted of the stories of a number of such girls, often from good families, given in their own words. It made heart-breaking reading. One told of how she had been out with a young man for an evening, and unwisely invited him in to her apartment for a cup of coffee late that night. There alone he prevailed upon her to give in to his demands. She spent the rest of the night sobbing bitterly in a chair, while he went contentedly to bed to sleep. I could not but visualize the sorrow and suffering that young man had caused not only to that poor girl, but to the respectable family from which she came, a sorrow that would last over the years. I found myself quite unable to count it all up. I have heard silly women in country parts call such babies "love babies." Their true name is rather "lust babies." True love sanctified by God does not produce the unhappiness that lust always does. Even the parents' forcing a couple in this situation to marry does not always repair the damage. Such marriages do not often turn out happily, and frequently the parents' desire that this should be done is born out of a wish to spare themselves disgrace, rather than out of concern for the highest good of the two involved. No, the real answer is the old one, that they repent and come to the Cross of the Lord Jesus as sinners, like every man who wants to be saved has had to do. Then the grace and love of God for such sinners comes in, the sin is forgiven, peace with God is restored, a testimony to His grace is on their lips, and if they are willing to do what He shows is to be done, He can overrule and recover the whole situation in such a way as will bring glory to Himself and grateful praises from the hearts of men. I know cases where the grace of God has done just that and has left nothing behind but songs of praise to "Him who loved us, and washed us from our sins in His own blood, and hath made us kings and priests unto God and his Father.''[1]

This grace can also reach another person grievously wronged in situations like these — the child growing up and going through life without a legal father, sometimes not even knowing him and all the time bearing the stigma of the term ''illegitimate.'' Such is the delicacy of the human make-up, this can have strange and even disabling psychological effects on the one who is the result of this illicit union, and that not only in youth but right on through life. I have known of those who have had difficulty in contracting a real marriage because of the psychological effects of doubts about their parentage. This is another of the forgotten factors. In all a man's or woman's repenting, let him or her be sure to repent deeply before God of the wrong done to that innocent son or daughter.

Of course where a child is happily adopted, these effects are greatly reduced. But today now that society is more ready to accept the unmarried mother, there are fewer and fewer babies being offered for adoption, as an increasing number of girls decide to keep their babies. But sooner or later the reproach and deprivation of it all is bound to catch up with the child and adolescent, with all the sense of loss and resentment that so often ensues.

This is not said to add to the remorse and self-recrimination of the one responsible, but rather the reverse. For when a sin with all its effects is brought in deep confession to the Cross of the Lord Jesus, the grace of God not only blots out the guilt of it, but extends even to one wronged by it. ''There is nothing too hard for Jesus, there is nothing that He cannot do,'' where the one responsible is found at His feet in penitence. He knows how to work in

1. Rev. 1:5-6.

that other life, healing the wounds and making all things new for that person. He can bring such a one to receive Him as his personal Saviour; there are then no further doubts about his parenthood, nor any sense of loss. He has God as his Father and he is a joint heir with Christ and the entail of his origin is gloriously broken.

5

THE FORGOTTEN FACTOR
OF MULTIPLIED DUPLICITIES

We halted the story of David at the point where he had committed adultery with Bathsheba without the knowledge of anybody but God and himself. We anticipated the coming of Nathan and heard him declare the factor of his sin, which David had forgotten but with which God was most concerned, the act of pillage against one of his common soldiers in taking his wife.

There is, however, more to follow in the story. Grievous as was his wrong in sparing to take of his own flock and taking the poor man's one lamb, what followed was even more grievous. I refer, of course, to the virtual murder of Uriah, Bathsheba's husband.

The common understanding on the part of those who have only a cursory knowledge of the Scripture records is that David had the husband put out of the way in order to possess himself of his wife, and that he was driven to this deed out of love and desire for Bathsheba. A closer reading of the story makes it clear that David's deed was far worse than this. He did not act out of love for anybody but himself. The story has not even the faintly redeeming feature of passionate desire for Bathsheba to be his wife.

The facts are these. David would have been quite content to have left the situation where it was, having enjoyed his secret moment of pleasure with Bathsheba, had she not informed him later that she had become pregnant. Uriah was not due home from the wars for many months, and if Bathsheba bore a child the secret would be out and David, the king, would be exposed. The situation was all the more grave in that the Mosaic law took the most serious view of adultery, even prescribing the death penalty for it, though it is uncertain as to how far this was always carried out. In order to cover his tracks David had Uriah sent back to him on the pretext of getting information as to the progress of the army operations. Having asked for news, David bade him to go to his home and spend the night with his wife. Had he done so, the child when it was born would have been thought to be Uriah's, which was exactly what David intended. But so devoted a soldier was Uriah that he preferred to sleep at the door of the king's house with David's other guards. In answer to David's question the next morning as to why he did not go to his home, he answered, "The ark, and Israel, and Judah abide in tents; and my lord, Joab, and the servants of my lord, are encamped in the open field. Shall I, then, go in to mine house, to eat and to drink, and to lie with my wife? As thou livest, and as thy soul liveth, I will not do this thing."[1]

Foiled in his attempt to hide what he had done, David tried again the next night, having him in to dine with him and making him drunk, being sure that then he would want his wife. But again Uriah prefers to sleep loyally with the other soldiers. David is desperate to cover his sin, and there now seems only one thing to do, to instruct his general to

1. 2 Sam. 11:11.

put Uriah in the most dangerous part of the battle where he is almost certain to lose his life, so that then David can take Bathsheba to be his wife and the child can be born in wedlock without anyone thinking that there had been improper relations before marriage. And so we have the pathetic sight of that loyal soldier carrying his own death sentence in that sealed letter. He had already proved his faithfulness and David knew he could trust him not to open it. In any case, he may well have been illiterate and unable to read it had he dared open it. All happened according to plan, nothing miscarried; Uriah was one of the first to fall in the next skirmish.

What David did he did not do out of any particular love for Bathsheba. She had been the instrument of a moment's pleasure and that was all she was to him. What he did was out of a concern for his own wretched self and reputation. To save himself from disgrace, he was prepared to have another man killed. He offered an innocent man up on the altar of his own reputation. In the light of all these moral undertones in the story, was there ever a more cynical and dastardly deed? But clear as it is to us as we read the story now, it was not yet clear to David. He had so rationalized everything, that he was quite blind to the fact that he was a virtual murderer. He knew there were certain wrongs he had committed, that he had been lecherous and overcome by his sex impulses, but he had not seen *murder*. His rationalization of this aspect of his conduct comes out in his comment, when the news of Uriah's death is conveyed to him by his general, Joab: ''Let not this thing displease thee, Joab, for the sword devoureth one as well as another.'' [2] It took the prophet Nathan to bring this forgotten factor to him, and it came as a shock to David to see it. Said Nathan,

2. 2 Sam. 11:25.

"Why hast thou despised the commandment of the Lord, to do evil in His sight? Thou hast killed Uriah, the Hittite, with the sword, and hast taken his wife to be thy wife, and hast slain him with the sword of the children of Ammon."[3]

Here we come to a further forgotten factor which is almost always present in sexual misbehavior, the multiplied duplicities to which a person has to resort to hide what he or she has done or is still doing. It is what the Bible calls "adding sin to sin."[4] To the sin of the actual sexual misbehavior and loose living has to be added the further sin of lies, deception, giving false impressions, play-acting, subterfuge, all to hide what has taken place or is still going on. In every situation of sexual misbehavior of which we have ever heard, we can always assume that there has been woven a vast web of lies and deception before it came fully into the light. The subterfuges may not have gone to the length that David's did (maybe if we had as much to lose as a king had we would not have acted any better); but the lies told to parents, the deceptions practiced on wife or husband, are every bit as culpable in the sight of God as what David did. May I ask, in all our repenting have we repented of *that?* And if God shows us, are we willing to put it right?

Today the telling of untruths to spare ourselves and save us from trouble is not considered wrong. It is not so with God. The Bible makes the most basic declaration about God when it says, "God is light, and in him is no darkness at all."[5] In the New Testament, the words "light" and "darkness" are not merely vague synonyms for good and evil. The light simply means that which reveals, whereas the darkness means that which hides. This will give new

3. 2 Sam. 12:9.   4. Isa. 30:1.   5. 1 John 1:5.

meaning to many a familiar passage. This declaration means that God is the all-revealing One; that all the time He is showing up everything to be just what it is, our motives and thoughts as well as our actions; and that with Him nothing can be hidden. Truthfulness must be the basis of our approach to Him. "Thou desirest truth in the inward parts."[6] But how foreign this is to us, who are naturally creatures of darkness. Rather than come to the light our natural reaction is to run away from it, because we have things to hide about ourselves; for "everyone that doeth evil hateth the light, neither cometh to the light, lest his deeds should be reproved."[7] Sometimes when one lifts a big stone, one sees a lot of little creatures, all of which are scrambling desperately for holes and cracks. They are creatures of darkness, at home in the dark, and when the light shines in and shows them all up, their only desire is to get into the dark again. Even so are the sons of men, irrespective of whether theirs are sexual sins or otherwise.

The passage that tells us that God is light and in Him is no darkness at all goes on to give promises of wonderful grace, if we are only willing "to walk in the light, as he is in the light"[8]— which of course is the reverse of hiding sin. First we are promised "fellowship one with another." That means that God can always have fellowship with the man who is completely honest about himself and his sin, no matter how grievous his sin may be. Honesty rather than holiness is the basic requirement in our relationship with God. Actually honesty about our unholiness is the first step into holiness. We all know that when a man says, "I have been terribly selfish over this and that," that it is the first step for him out of that selfishness. The simple truth is that God can do anything for a man who will not hide but

6. Ps. 51:6.   7. John 3:20.   8. 1 John 1:7.

be honest with Him. Furthermore, the words "one with another" also offer the possibility of fellowship with other people, for they cannot have true fellowship with a man who wears a mask. That is a gain indeed, for how shut off from other people we feel ourselves to be until we begin to be honest.

But more than fellowship is promised such a man. The verse goes on to say, ". . . and the blood of Jesus Christ, his Son, cleanseth us from all sin." The man who has come to God in true repentance and honesty about his sin has his heart and conscience washed whiter than the snow, and that by no less an agency than the blood of Jesus Christ. That precious blood speaks of the completed judgment-bearing of the Lord Jesus Christ on the cross of Calvary. There is nothing that the most tormented conscience can charge itself with, no sense of shame under which it may labor, but was anticipated and settled by the Son of God when He offered Himself for him on the cross. And God has declared Himself satisfied with what His Son did for the sins of the world in the most convincing way possible, in that He raised Him from the dead.

> "If Jesus had not paid the debt,
> He ne'er had been at freedom set."

And with the cleansing of His Blood goes all the other help and restoration, even as to our situations, which the grace of God has for us — but more of that in a later chapter.

Here then is another of the forgotten factors, the multiplied duplicities that sin always brings. May we find in the healing promises of the grace of God sweet inducements to repent even on these points.

6

FORGOTTEN FACTORS IN HOMOSEXUALITY

We must now face the matter of homosexuality, i.e., sexual relations between people of the same sex, men with men or women with women, and ask ourselves whether there are any forgotten factors here; that is, are there aspects which need repentance before God, which are not generally regarded as needing it?

Normal heterosexual people have a natural aversion to the thought of homosexual practice and would rather not even consider it. But it is a growing evil spreading through our society, and I fear increasing numbers of people are in danger of being drawn into it. Some of those we may want to help may be among that number, and therefore we must face it. Be assured, the grace of our merciful God has a perfectly adequate answer to this need, and He finds no more difficulty with this misbehavior than with the others we have mentioned. We can confidently assert, there is every hope for the homosexual in the Lord Jesus.

We must begin with the fact that today these actions have ceased to be regarded by many as sinful. They regard such things as unnatural and abnormal perhaps, but certainly not sins, that is, actions which are morally indefensible. They have lost sight of the fact that a holy God utterly condemns such practices. That is the forgotten factor. And the homosexual seeking help must begin here, or he does not begin at all.

The change in the public attitude has come about in this way: first, our legislators have decided to remove the practice of homosexuality as a crime from the statute books —though there are still clauses that seek to prevent those under a certain age from being corrupted. The publicity with which this has been accomplished has given the impression that it is now socially acceptable. It is only a short step from there for the impression to gain ground that it is not to be regarded as even sinful, that the Almighty Himself takes an indulgent view of the matter. This outlook can begin to seep into the thinking even of Christians.

It must be admitted that there is a difference between crime and sin. Crime is the transgressing of the laws of the state; sin is the transgressing of the laws of God. The state does not set out to govern and limit all the actions of men, only those that might prove harmful to others, that is, to society. The laws of the state leave men free to do as they like with the rest of their lives. Not so with the laws of God; men are accountable to Him for every part of their lives, their thoughts and motives as well as their actions. Things are forbidden, certainly, which inflict wrong on others, just as the state forbids them; but the laws of God go deeper here than the laws of the state do, and cover a wider area. But there is a whole range of things which the laws of God call transgression which have nothing to do with the harm they might do to others. They are wrong just because God is God and He says they are wrong. There are without doubt reasons why He says so, and He knows life works out best for men when they obey His laws. But we must not make our obedience to His laws contingent on our understanding how it is they are beneficent. We must obey just because God is the final moral arbiter and because He says what He does.

Now it was decided to alter the law of the land and make homosexual practices no longer criminal on the ground that it was a private matter for individuals, that it was not inflicting any harm on society, and therefore outside the control of the state. Moreover, it was argued that the law must be compassionate to people involved in this. But it is very much open to question that this activity does not harm society. Homosexual tendencies are not only congenital, that is, part of a man's original make-up which he cannot help; but they are more often acquired by one's being introduced to such practices by others. The practices to which he is introduced then cause all his sexual instincts to become perverted and twisted, running in an unnatural direction, with the result that he can be rendered incapable of the joys of a happy married life and children. And this can spread as a scourge through our communities, as it did through Sodom and Gomorrah. Can it be said that all people in those cities were congenital cases, born that way, and that nobody was therefore responsible? Hardly; their homosexuality was doubtless acquired through the practices being introduced from one to another, until there was an almost universal addiction. Had things been allowed to continue that way, the population would have declined and even died out for lack of normal families being set up. If that is not harm done to society, what is? True, the law in our country has provisions aimed at protecting those under a certain age; but it is not only those under a certain age who can be perverted.

So be it; our society is not to be protected from this thing, and the practice of homosexual acts is no longer a crime. But it is still sin — the laws of God have never been liberalized. And the first thing the homosexual caught in this problem must do if he wants God's help is to agree with Him and call it sin. This counsel might seem to be lacking in compassion and sympathy, and at variance with what some modern psychiatry would tell a man. But the Bible way is so often at variance with modern thought and when we encourage a man to call such a thing sin it is not to torture him with a deepened sense of guilt, but rather to assist him to take the first step toward deliverance. For if homosexuality is not sin, but simply an unfortunate trait in his make-up, he is stuck with it for life; there is nothing much that can be done about it, except to learn to live with it. Indeed, a psychiatrist said to me, ''We do not profess to cure a homosexual, but only to turn a miserable homosexual into a happy one.'' Perish the thought! But if a man is willing to call it sin, then there is every hope in the world for him; there is for him a Saviour whose blood cleanses from sin; and he will find that the acknowledgment of sin is a man's best qualification to meet that Saviour. He will find that Christ's redemption is custom-made for such a man as he is and His power is available to free him from everything he is willing to call sin.

In the light of the clear statements of the Bible there must be no rationalizations here as to the sinfulness of homosexuality. The Bible is our only text book as to the mind of God in the matter, and it is utterly clear. There is, first of all, the case of the cities of Sodom and Gomorrah and their utter destruction by God because of the prevalence of this sin. Then there is the passage in Romans 1, which speaks of ''the wrath of God revealed from heaven against all ungodliness and unrighteousness of men.''[1] It goes on to tell us some of the things that attract that wrath: ''for even their women did change the natural use into that which is against nature; and likewise also the men, leaving the natural use of the woman, burned in their lust one toward another; men with men working that which is unseemly, and receiving in themselves that recompence of their error which was meet.''[2] Then there is the passage in Corinthians to which allusion has already been made. The Authorized Version has it ''nor effeminate nor abusers of themselves with mankind . . . shall inherit the kingdom of God.'' For those two expressions ''effeminate . . . nor abusers of themselves with mankind'' (there are two words in the Greek too) the Revised Standard Version gives just one word, ''homosexuals,'' and that makes Paul's meaning quite clear to the modern mind; and he says that such shall not inherit the kingdom of God. In another place he says, ''for which things' sake the wrath of God cometh on the sons of disobedience.''[3] So the first thing the practicing homosexual who longs to be set free must do is confess that in playing with these things he has been playing with one of the things that bring the wrath of God upon the world of unbelievers.

It is at this point that we must be careful to understand what constitutes the sin to be repented of in the matter of homosexuality, otherwise we shall get ourselves and those we wish to help into bondage. A person's homosexual tendencies are his raw material. Most people have a normal

1. Rom. 1:18.   2. Rom. 1:26, 27.   3. Col. 3:6 (R.V.).

raw material, but with others it is a perverted raw material. The perverted raw material is in itself no more sinful than the normal one; the important thing is what one does with it. One can either indulge self in his raw material, contrary to the will of God, or deny self in his raw material. That means that fornication and a homosexual act are both equally sin. Both represent the indulging of self contrary to the will of God, the only difference being that the raw material with which each begins is different. If a man with homosexual tendencies indulges himself in those perverted desires, whether that indulgence is only in fantasy or in actual deed with another, that is sin. If a man, however, doggedly before God denies self in that raw material, repenting of the first responses in his heart and in his need looks to Jesus, that is the first step to holiness. What a beautiful thought — holiness for a homosexual! And that is the offered possibility in Jesus Christ, as we shall see in this and later chapters.

Let not therefore a man or woman feel condemned merely because he or she has this perverted raw material; it is what he does with it that matters. The tendency may be a congenital thing, having been with him since earliest years, and therefore he can hardly be blamed for it. On the other hand, it may be an acquired thing, through his own wrongdoing. In that case, he must humble himself to confess that wrong to God and be forgiven and cleansed from guilt completely — though the raw material may still be with him, of course. He is then in the same position as the other man, both of them with raw materials about which they need not despair or condemn themselves. Both are now given the opportunity to confess to God where they have not denied self but indulged self in that raw material, and come to the Cross of Jesus in faith in His promise that He forgives them their sin and cleanses them from all unrighteousness.[4] This will mean a clear and clean break with any wrong relationships with others, and a fleeing from situations of special temptation. At His feet they are not merely to ask His help with regard to any further temptations which their raw material may send up to their consciousness, but let Him take over the whole battle — indeed, their whole lives. There is all the difference in Jesus' merely being asked to help us and in His taking over. As they keep close to His Cross, repenting at any time of the first wrong movements of their hearts and bringing them to Him, they will find themselves being set free by the Lord; for the blood of Jesus keeps on cleansing us as we keep on coming to Him with the first beginnings of sin. I have known those who have been wonderfully helped by the Lord in this way, and they are today happily married with children. Others there have been who have not felt able to marry, but they are victorious nonetheless.

This is all very different from the way in which the practicing homosexual reasons. Because he feels he cannot have a sexual life in normal directions, he feels it to be his inalienable right to indulge himself in these perverted directions. But a man with normal desires does not usually reason that way. He or she may not be married; that satisfaction may not yet be granted to him — indeed it may never be. But he does not think *that* fact gives him the right to be promiscuous with every attractive person of the opposite sex he (or she) meets. He has to deny his natural impulses in order to be at least a respectable member of society, let alone a Christian.

Some homosexual may ask here, Does it mean then that I

4. 1 John 1:9.

am never to have sexual fulfillment? Yes, it may mean just that, unless and until God changes your raw material. Many a person has had to go through life without matrimony in any case. There was perhaps no other choice open to him, or perhaps he chose to remain single rather than marry one who was not God's choice for him. Such people have found nonetheless real fulfillment for their lives, even without sexual experience, and Jesus Christ has been to them all they needed, more than husband or wife. That is why you need the Lord Jesus as your Saviour, taking over your life from you and satisfying your heart, if you are going to get through to peace and deliverance. You will never make it otherwise. But if He is yours, you have everything else. He knows how to give a thousand cushions and compensations for your surrender of self's desires; and a life and ministry for others will open up that would not otherwise have been possible.

It may further be asked, Can He not quite change this wrong raw material for me, so that I no longer have this ding-dong battle within? Yes, indeed. He has done it for many, and they are enjoying a normal life today. But it is not likely to happen in your case unless you come to the place where you say, "Be my desires what they may, I am going to the Cross, there to deny them every time." Then He is able to do something about the raw material, either quite suddenly or progressively. If His will should be otherwise, you continue to walk with Him in the way of the Cross in peace.

I must hasten to add an important qualification to what has been said here about a perverted raw material, lest anyone who has indulged in some homosexual act might then think that that indicates he is of necessity an inveterate homosexual and is saddled for ever with a perverted raw material. There has been so much talk of late by psychiatrists and legislators on this subject that such a person might easily in despair class himself as one of those who can never contract a happy marriage and he thus becomes part of that lonely withdrawn group of people who struggle grimly with their tendencies, or finally indulge them. And all the time that may be far from the truth; he or she may not be an inveterate homosexual at all. Any normal heterosexual person could commit a homosexual act if he or she was defiant enough of the divine command and determined enough to have new sexual experiences.

The truth is that God does not call homosexuality by any other fancy name than sin and He invites the man concerned to do the same, and to find a wonderful door of hope for himself in doing so. For, as we have said, if it is sin there is a remedy in Christ for it, along with every other sin. Scripture does not put it in a special category needing special treatment, but simply classes it as sin with all manner of other sins. Indeed, the very passage in Romans quoted earlier, which speaks of women changing the natural use into that which is against nature and the men burning in their lust toward one another, goes on to describe people away from God as being filled with all unrighteousness, wickedness, covetousness, maliciousness, envy, murder, strife, deceit, and much besides. The whole lot is classed together as plain, straightforward sin, homosexual acts among them, and laid out before God as such; and if there is forgiveness and cleansing in the Lord Jesus for covetousness, malice, envy, murder, strife, and deceit, there is the same for this unnatural use of sex. Thank God, the Lord Jesus anticipated and settled for this sin and for every other sin "in his own body on the tree,"[5]

5. 1 Pet. 2:24.

and a fountain has been opened[6] to cleanse the stain of this sin as of every other sin. The answer then is to confess it to God as sin, and believe in His willingness and power to forgive you your sin, cleanse you from its defilement, set you free from its shame, and give sweet healing, either immediately or progressively, to whatever perversion there may be in your raw material.

The factors that we have mentioned with regard to the other forms of sexual misbehavior apply to this form of it too — the multiplied duplicities, and especially the wrong done to others. In practicing these things, a man has passed on to others the same perversion that he has. If it can be an acquired thing, then he has helped someone else to acquire it, he has ruined someone else's sexual life, and deprived someone else of the possibility of a happy domestic life. Even where this takes place between two apparently committed homosexuals, each still has to take the blame for the wrong done to the other; for no homosexual is irrecoverable, and each has pushed the other one just that bit further along the road and made his recovery so much harder.

These are the further matters over which repentance at the feet of Jesus is necessary if one is to know the full recovery of grace. Take time over this, dear one, seeing point by point the sinfulness of each forgotten factor and confessing it to Him. You will not have been humbling yourself long before the Lord ere you will find His peace stealing into your heart and you will know yourself forgiven, restored, and made whole. Then if He sends you to those other ones with whom you have sinned to ask their forgiveness too, He may well use your testimony to their restoration and healing also.

6. Zech. 13:1; 1 John 1:7.

7

THE DISHONOR DONE TO
ONE'S OWN BODY

I have hesitated to add a chapter on the wrong a man does to himself through sexual misbehavior, for people are usually only too conscious of the loss they have suffered and the unhappiness they have brought upon themselves through such actions, at least after the event. The losses men suffer extend from the loss of a good conscience with the uneasiness of always having something to hide, right up to the most excruciating and complicated situations when a man or woman sees all his happiness gone, it would seem, forever. Such wrongs that men do to themselves are hardly, therefore, forgotten factors; and in any case, a repentance based merely on those considerations would be prompted too much by selfish motives and hence largely invalidated. There is therefore little need to write on this aspect.

There is however a certain wrong that a man does to himself through sexual misbehavior which is forgotten, and can easily be slurred over when a man comes to God for His forgiveness and restoration. It is what I may call the dishonor he has done to his body.

We must first of all understand the exalted view that the

New Testament takes of our bodies. Paul says, "Know ye not that your body is the temple of the Holy Spirit, who is in you, whom ye have of God?"[1] When a man repents of his sin and receives Jesus Christ as His personal Saviour, his heart is cleansed by the blood of Christ and the Holy Spirit enters to dwell in his body, in order to direct the whole of his life. Paul would have us see what a tremendous thing it is that the Holy Spirit Himself, the Third Person of the Trinity, dwells within us. By this very fact our bodies are constituted His temple, and therefore are regarded as holy and separated for Divine use as was the temple of old at Jerusalem. This even has a bearing on the one who is not yet a believer. His body is not yet *actually* a temple of the Holy Spirit, but it is so *potentially,* for the opportunity to receive Christ as his Saviour is ever open to him; moreover the price of his redemption has already been paid and the title deeds of his body belong to Christ, even if he has himself not yet relinquished possession.

In view of this, any misusing of our bodies is a defiling of the temple of God, to which are attached the most solemn penalties. "If any man defile the temple of God, him shall God destroy; for the temple of God is holy, which temple ye are."[2] And all sexual misbehavior is just that, a defiling of the holy temple of God. It is a using of His temple for purposes other than those for which it was intended. The body that should have been used for the worship of God is used rather for the worship of the devil. What a terrible desecration! What a dishonor done to our bodies! The right modern word is to *abuse* the body. It is not without significance that the more familiar and older expression to describe masturbation is self-abuse, and that this term has been largely dropped for the more technical

1. 1 Cor. 6:19.   2. 1 Cor. 3:17.

word — presumably because people do not want to be reminded of the true nature of what they are doing. When a person goes in for this solitary sexual indulgence, he is abusing himself, he is using his body for a purpose for which God and nature never intended it should be used.

Paul in another place gives us an even more exalted view of our bodies. He loves to speak of the believer being joined to Christ through the Holy Spirit dwelling within him, as limbs are joined to a body. Christ is the head, we are His members joined to Him, with the same life from Him pervading us all. Listen then to the tremendous use he makes of this metaphor when he speaks of the wrong use of sex. "Do you not know that your bodies are members of Christ? Shall I therefore take the members of Christ and make them members of a prostitute? Never! Do you not know that he who joins himself to a prostitute becomes one body with her? For, as it is written, 'The two shall become one flesh.' But he who is united to the Lord becomes one spirit with Him.''[3] When a man goes into that apartment at the invitation of that doubtful girl, or into that "house of ill-fame,'' that brothel, he is taking that precious body of his, those members which are the members of Christ, and giving them over to the most debasing actions of all, making them part of a girl without principle and honor, a complete perversion of the high and holy purposes God intended.

What has been said of self-abuse and prostitution is equally true of all other forms of immorality, homosexuality, and perversion.

Hear, finally, Paul's further word on this, summing it all up, it seems: "Shun [fornication]. Every other sin which a man commits is outside the body; but the [fornicator]

3. 1 Cor. 6:15-16 (R.S.V. margin).

sins against his own body.''[4] Could anything be clearer that sexual misbehavior is a dishonor done to the body, which is the temple of God, the member of Christ? *The fornicator sins against his own body.*

In all our repenting, let us repent of this, and confess it to God, that we have dishonored our bodies. And for our encouragement let us think back to the Gospel record and remind ourselves that such is the grace of the Lord Jesus, that none received so ready a forgiveness as those who repented of immorality. The woman taken in adultery in John chapter 8 heard Him say, ''Neither do I condemn thee: go, and sin no more,''[5] while the hypocritical Pharisees who tried to accuse her to Him were left in the darkness of their own sin.

For our further encouragement let me point out that many of the saintly Christians in the church at Corinth were converts from these very practices. Paul certainly thunders out ''Be not deceived; neither fornicators, nor idolators, nor adulterers, . . . nor homosexuals, nor thieves, nor covetous, nor drunkards, nor revilers, nor robbers shall inherit the kingdom of God.'' But having said all this he joyfully adds, ''and such were some of you; *but*'' (what a glorious but!) ''ye are washed, but ye are sanctified, but ye are justified in the name of the Lord Jesus and by the Spirit of our God.''[6] The church at Corinth was a church of converted and delivered fornicators, adulterers, homosexuals, thieves, and drunkards. And why not? — that is what the church is meant to be, a bunch of sinners, saved by the grace of God!

A young man came up to me after a meeting in an American Christian college, in great distress. ''What is troubling me is this verse,'' he said, and he pointed to

4. 1 Cor. 6:18 (R.S.V.).   5. John 8:11.   6. 1 Cor. 6:9-11.

these words in his Revised Standard Version, ''nor homosexuals . . . will inherit the kingdom of God.''[7] ''That's me,'' he said, ''I cannot get into the kingdom of God then.'' ''But you must not stop there,'' I said, ''look at the next verse: 'but such were some of you, but ye are washed . . . sanctified . . . justified.' Repent deeply at the foot of the cross where Jesus will do all this for you and you are part of the same band of people — mighty sinners, saved by mightier grace.''

7. 1 Cor. 6:9-10.

8

THE GRIEVOUS WRONG
DONE TO GOD

We come now to the most basic of all wrongs in sexual misbehavior, but the one which is most forgotten — the wrong done to God. This was the aspect of his sin which David ultimately came to confess more than any other, for in his great psalm of penitence concerning the matter, he says, "Against thee, thee only, have I sinned, and done this evil in thy sight."[1] And yet it was something that David never saw until that day when Nathan came to him.

After the long sordid story is given us in detail, there comes at the end of the chapter this simple pregnant sentence, "But the thing that David had done displeased the Lord."[2] One reads with a sense of relief that there is a final moral arbiter who is concerned with the wrongs that are perpetrated against the innocent. But what is this displeasure of the Lord? Is it merely the displeasure of a law-giver whose laws have been disregarded? Or could it be somehow God regards Himself as having suffered a personal wrong in a matter like this? I believe it was the latter, though David was quite blind to it until his eyes

1. Ps. 51:4.   2. 2 Sam. 11:27.   55

were opened under Nathan's message.

These were the words in which the wrong done to God was revealed: "Thus saith the Lord God of Israel, I anointed thee king over Israel, and I delivered thee out of the hand of Saul; and I gave thee thy master's house, and thy master's wives into thy bosom, and gave thee the house of Israel and of Judah; and if that had been too little, I would moreover have given unto thee such and such things. Wherefore hast thou despised the commandment of the Lord, to do evil in His sight? thou hast killed Uriah the Hittite with the sword, and hast taken his wife to be thy wife."[3] What a catalog of the goodness of God toward David is recited to him! No one knew better than David how good God had been to him. Nathan's words reminded David how, while an obscure shepherd boy, the youngest in his family, he had been chosen by the distinguishing grace of God to be God's next king of Israel and anointed there in the presence of the family by Samuel. These words reminded David of the bitter jealousy and hatred he had endured for years from the reigning king, Saul, of how on numbers of occasions he had been within an ace of death at his hands, and of how God had delivered him again and again. He was reminded of how this persecuted young man had, first, Judah turn to him as their king, and later the whole house of Israel, and all that without his having to lift a finger to achieve it — it came to him as the gift of God. He was pointed to all the wealth God had given him, and even all the adequate provision for his sexual satisfaction which had been granted him. Then further he is told (and poor David is getting lower and lower under this recital) that if in spite of all this generosity he had thought this was not enough, it was in God's heart to give him yet more. No

3. 2 Sam. 12:7-9.

one had been dealt with more generously by God than David, and he knew it.

Then came the searching words that cut their way right into his heart, "Wherefore then hast thou despised the commandment of the Lord?" In other words it was as if He said, "When so much was given you, why must you snatch at the one small fruit that was denied you — another man's wife — as if I had been grudging to you, as if I was not willing to give you yet more, as if I did not know what was best designed for your happiness, as if I did not really love you?" There seems to be a wail in those words, for in them stands revealed all the deep hurt that God had suffered through David's sin. That finished David. There was no attempt at hiding, excuses, or self-justification. In that moment he broke before God and in one short sentence he uttered the most important words any man can utter, "I have sinned against the Lord."[4] And when afterward as a restored man he wrote his testimony in that psalm already referred to, it was this aspect of his sin and of God's forgiveness of it that gripped his heart and mind.

So often there is this element present in a man's sexual misbehavior, if he only has eyes to see it. The sexual offences of men and women have not always been committed because they lacked anything. Their sin has been so often committed against the backdrop of the goodness and generosity of God to them. How good God is to men! That young single man or woman had been given so much — good parents, a happy home, an adequate prosperity, bright prospects, and who knows what good thing God had planned for him in the future, for His goodness extends to all His creatures, whether they acknowledge Him or not. There was no need for that

4. 2 Sam. 12:13.

young man or woman to snatch at that unripe fruit. They had only to wait God's time, and He would have given them all that was in His will for them, a beloved life-partner, a home of their own, a happy family, and all the gratification of their sex desires that was right — and all that without bitterness or guilty secrets. But no, he or she must snatch at the one fruit that was forbidden, as if God was grudging, as if He would never give them what they craved unless they grabbed at some paltry opportunity quickly. And in so doing, great wrong has been done to God. And what is true of the unmarried is even more true of the married. So much was given them by a good God; husband or wife, children, laughter, home. Nobody thought that that home would break up, but it did. Whatever the reason, it was not because God had not been good to them, not because He was not prepared to be yet more good to them. But it was the greed of man and his distrust in the goodness of God that made him snatch at forbidden fruit — and no one has been hurt more in the process than God.

The method that Satan used to get our first parents to commit the first sin was precisely along this line. He said, "Hath God said, Ye shall not eat of every tree° of the garden?"[5] In those words he took their eyes off the many trees of which they could eat — and what a profusion there was of them — and sought to fix them on the one tree of which they could not eat. And he continued to do so (and I doubt not that this temptation was something insistent and continuous over perhaps a long period), until at last they felt they were martyrs, with no liberty at all, hemmed in on every side — all because of that one tree

5. Gen. 3:1.

whose fruit they were not allowed to eat. Matthew Henry in his comment on this put it this way in his courtly English, ''The devil by aggravating the exception, endeavoured to invalidate the concession. The divine law cannot be reproached unless it first be misrepresented.''

Is that not Satan's method with all of us? He takes our eyes off the many good things God has given us, and fixes our eyes on the things that are forbidden us — the pretty face we are not to stare at, the person about whom we are forbidden to indulge sexual thoughts, the ones to whom we are to make no advances. And he so fixes our eyes on what is forbidden that we are ultimately ripe for rebellion against the moral laws that seem to cramp us on every side — forgetful of the many other trees, the wide profusion of them, that God has granted us.

Satan, however, went further. Having suggested that the prohibition was unreasonable and limiting, he then proceeded to malign the One who made it, God Himself. He suggested that He had hidden motives in refusing them this tree. Making use of the name of the tree, the Tree of the Knowledge of Good and Evil, he said, ''God doth know that in the day ye eat thereof . . . ye shall be as gods, knowing good and evil.''[6] In other words, he said, ''The reason God forbids you to eat of that tree is that He does not want you to know too much, He does not want you to be a god like Himself, He wants to keep you down, He is not willing for your highest good; so you had better take things into your own hands.'' He was playing the same part as the communist agitator does today, but in a higher and more dangerous sphere. And this went on until Eve's heart became hardened against God and she felt that to do what was proposed was only self-defence. How modern the

6. Gen. 3:5.

Bible is! Is not this the story behind so many falls, of the solicitations to sin that have so often entered the mind? A girl who has been denied sexual experience feels that she never will have any unless she accepts the opportunity afforded by this man who is urging her. After all, life has been hard on her. God has not given her what He has given to others; He seems to have forgotten her; she had better take things into her own hands. And the same is true of every other class of person, the homosexual as well as the heterosexual, each in his different category.

And the greatest loser in it all is God, the One whose heart was so different toward them from what they thought, the One who was planning such good, greater than they had imagined — but whose purposes of love they have spoiled. How much a man must be pained when on returning from a business trip abroad he finds that someone has been poisoning the minds of his wife and children against him, and that now instead of running to meet him, they run from him, and indeed take up sticks against him, being quite sure that if they do not hit him first, he will hit them. Actually I do not need to invent illustrations. I once stayed in a home where the two children were gripped with the fear that their parents were not going to feed them adequately. It was so strong in them that it must have been some unusual psychological condition. As each meal time came round there was great anxiety whether there would be any food prepared for them, and they were forever going into the kitchen to make sure that mother was preparing the dinner. Even so they were always doubtful whether mother was going to put the sugar in and whether she was not going to skimp on their food. What a painful experience it was for those parents! One could imagine that if that condition went on unchecked the children might one day do some dreadful thing against their parents, on the assumption that their parents were against them. All of this illustrates the bitter wrong done against God when men allow themselves to believe the thoughts that Satan puts into their minds and proceed to take things into their own hands.

Is not this yet another of the forgotten factors in sexual misbehavior, and the most important — the wrong done against God and His goodness? If a man is to know a restored peace with God he will have to get at last to the low place where David got and say with him, "Against thee, thee only, have I sinned, and done this evil in Thy sight."[7]

Perhaps there is no greater hymn of penitence with regard to this aspect of things than the lines penned by Sir H. W. Baker:

"God made me for Himself to serve Him here,
  With love's pure service and with filial fear;
To show His praise, for Him to labour now;
  Then see His glory where the angels bow.

All needful grace was mine through His dear Son,
  Whose life and death my full salvation won;
The grace that would have strengthened me and taught;
  Grace that would crown me when my work was wrought.

And I poor sinner, cast it all away;
  Lived for the toil or pleasure of each day;
As if no Christ had shed His precious blood,
  As if I owed no homage to my God.

O Holy Spirit, with Thy Fire divine,
  Melt into tears this thankless heart of mine;
Teach me to love what once I seemed to hate
  And live to God before it is too late."

7. Ps. 51:4.

Can you not hear in these words the sob of the man who sees he has sinned against the goodness of God and His high purpose for him? And are not these the words you might well use yourself as you come back to the Lord?

9

AMAZING GRACE —
THE MESS UNMESSED!

The purpose of God in all His dealings with sinners is not their condemnation and destruction, but rather their restoration and recovery. This is the sphere in which the Lord Jesus Christ excels — and He does that as much in the realm of sex failure as in any other. Indeed so great is His work of forgiveness, recovery, and restoration that the new thing He produces out of the wreckage of our sin after we have repented is sometimes better and sweeter than the original thing we so grievously spoiled. For this reason, in heaven there will be no vain regrets, no remorse, no "would-that-it-had-been-otherwise," for the work of restoration that grace has wrought for us and our lives will be seen to be complete and all-inclusive. As we look back we shall see that the Divine Potter has made again the vessel that we marred into another vessel, "as seemed good to the potter to make it,"[1] and has got infinite glory to Himself in so doing. Every last tear will be wiped away from our eyes and only a song of praise left to us. The wonderful thing is, however, that we can have those tears dried now and begin our song of praise now.

1. Jer. 18:4.

> "Ransomed, healed, restored, forgiven,
> Who like thee His praise should sing?"

Nowhere is the grace that "forgives the messer and unmesses the mess" more clearly seen than in the history of David. His story is given on the page of Scripture not so much to show a king who sordidly sinned but a God who wondrously forgave and restored. Indeed so great has been the restoration of grace that what should have been a continuing liability and disgrace to the Church, the fact that its greatest psalmist fell so shamefully, has been transmuted to become one of its greatest assets. No one's testimony has given contrite sinners such cause for encouragement and hope as David's, which he wrote out in full in Psalms 32 and 51. I like to think of him saying, as he handed the completed sheets to his chief singer, "Teach it to the people and sing it in the temple, and let all the world know the mercy that God has shown to a sinner like me." And the grace of God still turns our liabilities into assets, chief of which is the asset of a testimony that will encourage other sinners to receive Jesus Christ as we have — that is, if we are prepared to hold it at the disposal of God for this purpose.

The first thing we see is that David repented, and did so deeply on all the scores we have mentioned in these pages. As soon as Nathan faced him with God's message, he humbled himself before the prophet without a moment's evasion or self-excuse, and said, "I have sinned against the Lord."[2] The depth of his repentance can be gauged by the fact that he was willing to write out his testimony, the testimony of a forgiven sinner, and have it sung in the temple. How different was he from his predecessor, King

2. 2 Sam. 12:13.

Saul, who when he was challenged by the prophet Samuel, said the same words, "I have sinned," and then showed how insincere his repentance was by adding, "yet honour me now, I pray thee, before the elders of my people,"[3] i.e., do not let anybody know, go through the religious ceremonies with me. David on the other hand was willing to be known for what he really was, a sinner on whom God had had mercy. Then, too, the depth of his repentance is shown by the fact that in his psalm of testimony, Psalm 51, there are no evasions, no rationalizations of his sin, no saying what he had before, "the sword devoureth one as well as another."[4] Rather he writes, "Deliver me from bloodguiltiness, O God, thou God of my salvation."[5] He calls his sin what it is, murder. There were doubtless many around him ready to take his part, to persuade him that it was not really murder. But now that David has humbled himself before God, he will have nothing of it. He names himself a murderer and simply asks the Judge of all the earth for a reprieve.

If it be asked how David came by such honesty and self-judgment, it can only be answered that he knew the God he was dealing with, that He was a God merciful and gracious and ready to pardon. Standing before that grace, David knew that he could afford to confess the full extent of his sinfulness. And sure enough, quick as a flash, the answer came back, "The Lord also hath put away thy sin; thou shalt not die."[6] But notice that word "also." It was as if Nathan said, "In your confession and self-judgment you have put away your sin, that is, turned away from it. The Lord also has done the same. It can now be regarded as gone forever." The magnanimity of it should astonish us.

3. 1 Sam. 15:30. 4. 2 Sam. 11:25.
5. Ps. 51:14. 6. 2 Sam. 12:13.

"Oh matchless kindness, and He shows,
This matchless kindness to His foes."

And although the situation resulting from his sin is at the moment far from resolved, and although he has to undergo severe disciplines, he walks through them all now as a forgiven man in fellowship with God, and experiences all the comforts and sustainings of God.

The same grace is for us, when we repent as David did. Indeed for us that grace has been more manifest and made more certain, in that we know that while we were still in our sins, He gave His Son to die for us on the cross. The moment we cease to stiffen our necks, and bow our heads before the Lord Jesus in repentance and confession, that moment we hear the word, "The Lord also hath put away thy sin." As G. Campbell Morgan says in his comment on this scripture, "A man puts away his own sin when in sincerity he confesses it. That makes it possible for God *also* to put it away. The Divine putting away of sin is always made possible potentially by the Divine atonement; but it can become possible only in the experience of the sinner, when the sinner confesses, and so judges and puts it away from himself."*

And we have really got to believe that if God has put it away, it really is gone. "As far as the east is from the west, so far hath he removed our transgressions from us."⁷ The distance between the east and west is an infinite distance, a distance that in the nature of the case cannot be measured. Just as far has God put away the sins of the man who has repented. And although, as in David's case, the situation that we have caused by our sin continues for the time and

*From *Searchlights from the Word* by G. Campbell Morgan. Oliphants Ltd., London.
7. Ps. 103:12.

may involve us in many humbling disciplines, we may walk through them all as forgiven men, in fellowship with Jesus. Sometimes the fact that our sin leaves us with a painful entail, which is perhaps ever before us, may make it difficult for us to believe in, or at least to enjoy, the forgiveness of sins. But we must do so, or else dishonor God and the blood of His Son shed for us, for "he that believeth not God hath made him a liar."[8] And as we do so, God is able to transfigure the entail of our sin, so that it no longer bears the character of a judgment on us, but simply becomes God's raw material in which He is working out a new plan for our lives. But more of that in a moment.

David not only repented, but he submitted without question to all the disciplines that God laid upon him because of his sin. This in turn evoked a further marvelous grace from God, in addition to the marvel of His forgiveness.

Although God's forgiveness was utterly complete, God none the less imposed upon David heavy disciplines. First, Nathan had to say immediately after telling him that the Lord had put away his sin, "Howbeit, because by this deed thou hast given great occasion to the enemies of the Lord to blaspheme, the child also that is born unto thee shall surely die."[9] He was also told, "Now therefore the sword shall never depart from thine house; . . . Behold, I will raise up evil against thee out of thine own house. . . ."[10] These two things surely came to pass, and it is a touching sight to see the submissiveness and meekness of David under the chastenings of his God. He knew that "whom the Lord loveth he chasteneth, and scourgeth every son whom he receiveth."[11] He knew that the stroke that was falling upon

8. 1 John 5:10.   9. 2 Sam. 12:14.
10. 2 Sam. 12:10-11.   11. Heb. 12:6.

him was not the punishment of a judge, but rather the discipline of a father who had forgiven him, and he submitted to it as such, without quibble.

The details of the story may bear repeating. The child whom Bathsheba bore became ill. "David therefore besought God for the child; and David fasted, and went in, and lay all night upon the earth."[12] When however he heard the news that the child was dead, instead of being more cast down, he "arose from the earth, and washed, and anointed himself, and changed his apparel, and came into the house of the Lord, and worshipped: then he came to his own house; and when he required, they set bread before him, and he did eat."[13] When his servants expressed astonishment at his actions, he replied in noble words, "While the child was yet alive, I fasted and wept: for I said, Who can tell whether God will be gracious to me, that the child may live? But now he is dead, wherefore should I fast? can I bring him back again? I shall go to him, but he shall not return to me."[14] See here his uncomplaining submission to what God had allowed to come upon him.

Nathan's prophecy with regard to trouble arising to David from his own family certainly came to pass too. The darkest moment in David's life was when he learned that his own son Absalom had rebelled against him and had succeeded in alienating the whole nation from him and had usurped his throne.

The darkness of that sad night when David had to flee into exile with a few hundred faithful men was brightened, however, by this one ray, that all this was happening as God said it would, that although he was being squeezed, and squeezed very painfully, it was being done by the fingers of the God who had forgiven him and whom he had

12. 2 Sam. 12:16. 13. 2 Sam. 12:20. 14. 2 Sam. 12:22-23.

come to love. For that reason he did not find it hard to submit to the pressure of those fingers. When his followers wanted to take the ark of God with them, as the outward sign that God was on their side, David said, ''Carry back the ark of God into the city: if I shall find favour in the eyes of the Lord, he will bring me again, and show me both it, and his habitation: but if he thus say, I have no delight in thee; behold, here am I, let him do to me as seemeth good unto him.''[15]

This submission to God in the situation worked itself out also in an attitude of non-retaliation to others. When one of his old enemies cursed him openly as he fled, whom his followers would have struck down dead for his temerity, David said, ''Let him alone, and let him curse; for the Lord hath bidden him. It may be that the Lord will look upon mine affliction, and that the Lord will requite me good for his cursing this day.''[16] Nowhere was this attitude of gentleness and non-retaliation more demonstrated than in his attitude to his son, Absalom, the cause of all his sufferings. When ultimately David sent his men against Absalom and his forces, he was careful to instruct them, ''Deal gently for my sake with the young man, even with Absalom.''[17] His purpose was not that he should be slain, but that he should be brought back alive, that his father might love him into obedience. There is no more poignant cry of grief anywhere in literature than when he later heard that his son had been killed in the battle: ''O my son Absalom, my son, my son Absalom! would God I had died for thee, O Absalom, my son, my son!''[18] And this forbearance toward his enemies was due to the fact that he had first humbled himself before God and was taking the

15. 2 Sam. 15:25-26.　　16. 2 Sam. 16:11-12.
17. 2 Sam. 18:5.　　18. 2 Sam. 18:33.

situation as from His hand. And so it was that God not only forgave David but used all the sufferings and disciplines which were the entail of his sin to further him in the path of sainthood and submission to Himself.

With us too, although we may know ourselves forgiven, there may be deep disciplines which God may lay upon us, through the very situations which may come to us as the entail and consequence of our sins arising from them. To these disciplines of God we are called upon to submit without reservation or quibble, blaming no second causes, but seeing everything as coming to us from the loving hand of the God who has forgiven us. Only so shall we find this further grace that deals with the situation in which we find ourselves, and makes it the raw material for a fresh purpose of love.

Sometimes this submission can be lacking on the part of those who profess to have repented. I once heard of a man who had fallen into immorality, and whom the deacons of the Baptist church of which he was a member felt they must discipline in accordance with the Scriptures. His name was accordingly taken off the list of members and he was forbidden to partake of the bread and the wine in the communion services of the church, though they were glad for him to continue to attend the church services if he chose. He made a full confession and appeared to be repentant. He continued to attend the church and sat at the back of the communion services without partaking. Because the church did not soon reinstate him on the ground that he had confessed, he became indignant at what he called their unforgiving attitude and joined another church. This only served to show that the church was right in not giving him a speedy reinstatement. A truly repentant man would have submitted to all that might have been laid upon him — and for as long as his brethren thought necessary. He should have said, ''If they exclude me forever, it is only a little of what my sin really deserves,'' and he would have taken it from the hand of his God, and been at peace. That is the man who is soon acknowledged in the circle of the sinner's fellowship, which is what a Christian church really is. But if we do not find ourselves met with the forgiveness and understanding of others, it may be we have not repented truly enough and have not submitted deeply enough to all that may come upon us. Instinctively people feel it and treat us accordingly. It is very difficult not to forgive a truly broken man. And yet if people do treat us like that, in spite of all our self-abasement, it provides something more for us to go on submitting to, because first of all we are submitting to our God.

As David submitted to all that God allowed to fall upon him, he found God working on his behalf, taking up his affairs, vindicating him as His own child, silencing all his enemies. The very situation arising out of his sin was now no longer David's responsibility, but God's. It had now become the raw material for God's new purpose for David, in which He was going to show what a God David had, as if there was no blame attaching to David for the situation — and indeed there was no blame, for God's forgiveness of David was complete. This is not the place to rehearse all the details of the immortal story except to say that God delivered him from all his enemies and ultimately brought him back to the very throne which one would have thought he had justly forfeited forever. Absalom was slain in battle, his army routed, and later the whole nation sent David the message, ''Return thou, and all thy servants.''[19]

19. 2 Sam. 19:14.

And David ends more loved and honored than ever before, his throne more secure, and his kingdom more prosperous. And the experiences through which he had passed of his own failure, the hatred of bitter enemies, and God's infinite restoring grace now only furnish the ''sweet psalmist of Israel'' with matter for further songs of praise to God. What an illustration all this is of the fact that God not only forgives the repentant one, but takes up cudgels if necessary on his behalf, owning him before all as His child and servant.

The same applies to us. Till we repent, the situation which we have created for ourselves is our responsibility. But from the moment when we humble ourselves in repentance and confession, the situation becomes God's, and His purpose is to work something new in it. As with David, it is now simply His raw material for a new plan of love as if there were no blame attaching to us. The responsibility is transferred from our shoulders to His, and He bids us rest in Him about it all, and then simply co-operate with Him by obeying the light He gives us as to the next steps to be taken. And as we do so, He works on our behalf, and a new pattern begins to emerge, which bears unmistakable marks of His hand, and we find Him bringing order out of chaos, as we walk with Him in peace. And if we ask how it is possible to walk with Him in peace in the midst of situations of difficulty to which our sins have so greatly contributed, I reply that we cannot be washed whiter to the eye of God than the blood of Christ washes us when we call sin, sin; and God is forever on the side of such a repentant man, even if he has been the worst sinner out of hell.

Such triumphs of grace are seen in great profusion and infinite variety wherever the gospel of Christ is proclaimed.

Many ranks of witnesses would rise to tell of the mighty grace that has forgiven them, remade them, and transmuted all the damage their sin had created, and done "better unto them than at their beginnings."[20] One such instance must suffice here. A young unmarried mother of my acquaintance found the Lord Jesus as her personal Saviour amid the ruins of her life. Not only on the score of her particular misbehavior but on every other score she saw herself a sinner, but one whom Jesus came to save. Being forgiven much, she loved her Saviour much, and learned to walk with Him moment by moment every day. So complete was the forgiveness and cleansing from sin which the Lord Jesus gave her that she was delivered from all sense of shame, and was left simply with a sinner's peaceful testimony to her Saviour. She became radiant, and bravely went to work, bringing up her child whom she now joyfully accepted as God's gift to her — though not without sometimes having to return to the foot of the Cross when Satan reproached her with the past. She never wanted to be known other than what she really was and was always ready to give her testimony of the saving grace of Jesus to an unmarried mother. So she continued for some years. Then one day, as a Christian man sought God's mind as to his life partner, he was directed and drawn to her. Today they are married and another Christian home has been erected from which many praises ascend to God. And all that out of ruins, which for others away from God would have meant nothing but despair and cynicism. Make no mistake, when God is allowed to get into a life, there is *always* a happy ending, no matter what the condition of things He may find when He comes.

David's confidence in the grace of God to a sinner was

20. Ezek. 36:11.

quite extraordinary, even when his sufferings were most directly related to his sin, and at their greatest intensity. I quote one incident for our own encouragement. The heading of the third psalm tells us that it was written by David "when he fled from Absalom his son." This was surely one of the darkest moments of his life, presumably made all the more so by the knowledge that Nathan had told him that this was one of the things that would come upon him as a discipline for his sins. One would have expected, therefore, to find David crushed in spirit and full of self-condemnation, quite sure that God was against him to give him what he deserved, and running away like a little dog with his tail between his legs. In actual fact the opposite was the case. We find him full of confidence in God, and utterly assured that God was on his side. Listen to him, "Lord, how are they increased that trouble me! many are they that rise up against me. Many there be which say of my soul, There is no help for him in God. *But thou, O Lord, art a shield for me; my glory, and the lifter up of mine head.*"[21] He continues in this vein, getting more and more confident until he ends by anticipating in faith the Lord's complete victory on his behalf and the utter routing of his enemies. "Arise, O Lord; save me, O my God; for thou *hast* smitten all mine enemies upon the cheek bone; thou *hast* broken the teeth of the ungodly."[22]

What an encouragement to any man today who is having to walk a difficult path because of the entail of his past wrongdoing! Such a man may have even greater cause for confidence in the God of grace than David because he can see that Jesus died for him and that His blood is mightily sufficient to cleanse every stain and remove completely the element of guilt over what has happened. There need be

21. Ps. 3:1-3.   22. Ps. 3:7.

therefore no further self-recrimination, no sense that God is taking a stick to him, but rather that God is on the side of the contrite one, making something new and beautiful out of the confusion he has caused. Meantime, He is using the intervening trials and disciplines as a means to hasten him on the path of sainthood and submission to Himself, as He did with David.

> "Something beautiful, something good;
>   All my confusion He understood;
> All I had to offer Him was brokenness and strife,
>   But He made something beautiful of my life."*

Something Beautiful © copyright 1971 by William J. Gaither. Used by permission.

10

DEEPER REPENTANCE

In the preceeding chapters you will have noticed one word has kept recurring, a word to which great importance seems to have been attached. Indeed, it has been emphasized that a true experience of the grace of God in restoration is dependent on it. It is the little word "repentance." It is important therefore that we should define it and make clear what is required of us here. Indeed, the mere fact that the subtitle of this book is "An aid to deeper repentance" makes it the more necessary to do so. For this we must turn to the Scriptures.

Any book of reference will tell us that the Greek word translated "repent" means to change one's mind. It is used to express a change of mind not only with regard to sin, but with regard to anything else. It is said that God "is not a man, that He should repent,"[1] that is, He does not change His mind. Again, "the gifts and calling of God are without repentance,"[2] which means that He does not change His mind with regard to the calling He has given us. Yet again, Esau "found no place of repentance, though he sought it carefully with tears."[3] This does not

1. 1 Sam. 15:29.   2. Rom. 11:29.   3. Heb. 12:17.

mean that Esau could not repent, but that he could not get his father, Isaac, to repent; that is, change his mind. Isaac had given his patriarchal blessing with all the goods that went with it to Jacob and he was not going to reverse it.

Usually, however, the word is used of man changing his mind with regard to moral issues. Where he said he was right, he admits himself to be wrong; where he justified himself, he now condemns himself. That is a costly change of mind indeed, for we all hate to be wrong and love to be right.

It seems we can summarize the calls of God for man to repent under three heads. First, he is called to "repentance toward God."[4] That is the basic repentance to which all sinners are called. They must repent of running their own lives and going their own way independent of God, and thinking it right to do so. They must change their minds, admit they are wrong in what they are doing, and turn to God. It is not a matter of confessing they have slipped off the highway of holiness on this or that matter, but rather of acknowledging they have never been on it at all but on the broad road that leads to destruction.

Then there is repentance of individual sins and attitudes, as when Peter said to Simon the sorcerer, "Repent therefore of this thy wickedness, and pray God, if perhaps the thought of thy heart may be forgiven thee."[5] This is a repentance to which not only the one who is turning to God for the first time is called, but also the Christian as need may occasion. The Lord's message to no less than five of the seven churches to whom He sent letters in the early chapters of Revelation was "Repent." (Rev. 2:5; 2:16; 2:21; 3:3; 3:19).

4. Acts. 20:21.   5. Acts 8:22.

Thirdly, we have the phrase "repentance from dead works."[6] I presume this phrase means seeking peace with God "not by faith, but as it were by the works of the law."[7] We must change our minds with regard to trying to earn our way back to God by the things we do. This may seem so right to us, but we must repent of such works and see they are dead and worthless to God unless we first come to Him by the new and living way of the blood of Jesus.

Repentance, then, is a change of attitude with regard to these three things; but we are thinking here especially with regard to the second, namely, sin. Repentance of sin must be expressed and it is done so in word by confession and in action by restitution.

First, confession. It must follow repentance, of course. We cannot confess as sin that which we have not repented of, but what we have repented of we must now confess. This confession is made primarily to God. It is not enough to say, "God knows all about it, why do I need to confess it to Him?" He says "Take with you words, and turn to the Lord."[8] You must therefore express your repentance in words. Get to your knees and start down the line telling God what you have done, what you now see the sin to be, and how it reveals you to be the man you are. Do not hurry over it. Take sides with God against yourself. You can call yourself all the bad names you like, and you will only be barely getting near the truth. I remember how once I had been repenting about myself before God, and had said some pretty hard things about myself. I felt I had been rather gracious about it all, perhaps had rather exaggerated the statement of my sinfulness, and I half expected God to say to me what one's fellows sometimes say when one takes the humble place: "I don't think you are as bad as all that."

6. Heb. 6:1.   7. Rom. 9:32.   8. Hos. 14:2.

Instead of that, as I rose that day, it was as if I heard heaven utter a great corroborating "Amen!"; in other words, "That's right!" Maybe we have been sparing ourselves here and our repentance needs to go deeper.

There are times when quite obviously this confession needs also to be made to man, to the one or ones we have wronged or deceived, and God will lead us as to how and when this should be done. This invariably involves us in losing our righteousness, that is, our reputation before others; and well that it does. Jesus lost His reputation for us when He took our place on the cross; and should we not be willing to cast ours away when He convicts us? It is of course a real death to do so, but in the Christian life we die to live, and how abundant the life — His life — that comes to us out of the grave of self! Maybe here, too, we need to go deeper and part with the last shred of our justification of ourselves.

Then repentance is expressed in action by restitution, or making reparation for the loss we have inflicted on others. There are cases where the only reparation we can make is to ask another's forgiveness. Often, however, we must go further; a thing stolen must be returned, a wrong relationship with another terminated, a decision taken must be reversed, a course embarked upon must be abandoned, an idol which has taken Christ's place in our lives must be given up. Sometimes generous reparation for losses inflicted should be made, as in the case of Zacchaeus, who more than repaid what he had defrauded people of. Though I have used the words "must" and "should," restitution is not to be made merely as a legal obligation, but because the heart has been reached and softened by the forgiveness of the Lord Jesus; and we now have His love for those people; and it is far more "I want to do it" than "I ought to."

Jesus said to the church in Laodicea, ''Be zealous therefore, and repent.''[9] Our teachers have rightly told us we ought to be zealous in witnessing, zealous in praying, zealous in reading our Bible. But it is as is Jesus says to us in this verse, ''Before all these others, be zealous in repenting.'' He wants us to repent in style, even as Zacchaeus did, wholeheartedly and with open hands.

The sign of a true confession is that it is made voluntarily and not only when we are found out — when we have little option but to confess. Achan's confession of sin with regard to the stealing of the gold and the garments in the overthrow of Jericho was of this order, and it brought him no forgiveness.[10] God gave him chance after chance to confess his sin voluntarily, as lots were cast, first between the tribes, then between the families in the tribe that was taken, then between the households in the family that was taken and then ultimately between the individuals. What a dramatic story it is! God could easily have told Joshua the name of the guilty man at the start and they could immediately have gone to his tent and found the stuff. But God deliberately chose to go this slow roundabout way to discover the guilty man, in order to give him the opportunity to make a voluntary confession that He might have mercy on him. But although the noose was being slowly tightened around Achan with each successive casting of the lots, he determined to bluff it out to the end, banking all the time that the final lot would not fall on him. When at last the household that was taken had to come man by man for that final lot, it was too late for mercy. He had demonstrated his stiff neck and unwillingness to repent right to the end, and although when faced with it he did

9. Rev. 3:19.   10. Josh. 7.

confess, the Divine edict was that he was to be stoned without reprieve.

Some people think they have done a wonderful thing if they own up when at last the matter is found out. But as long as there was a chance that it would never be discovered, they were content to go on in silence. Therefore their confession of sin, when at last it was made, was no real confession at all and did not bring to them the forgiveness of God. The confession of sin that moves the compassion of God and brings Him into a man's affairs is that of the man who confesses even if it would never be found out, when he does so moved only by the convictions and compellings of the Holy Spirit. It will need something more than the ''Achan'' confession of sin to bring a man into peace with God and to cause God to work on his behalf. And yet it does happen sometimes in life that the experience of being found out produces in a man, through the working of the Holy Spirit, a true self-judgment that brings him to God.

In the light of this we could have wished that David had not waited for Nathan to challenge him with his sin before he confessed it. How much more glorifying to God it would have been if David in the misery of his heart had sought out the prophet first and laid bare the whole story and asked his prayers. From this point of view one might doubt the genuineness of David's repentance. I have said that it needs something more than the Achan confession of sin to bring a man into peace with God. In David's case there certainly was this ''something more,'' otherwise David would never have known God's restoration in the way he did. I say this for the encouragement of any whose deceitful hearts have led them to defer their confession until they had no other option, and who therefore may be inclined to despair.

There is encouragement even for such from the story of David, for if there is found the ''something more'' in our repentance that there was in David's, we too may be assured of mercy. There were certainly other elements in David's repentance than the tardiness of his confession. First, the challenge of Nathan was welcomed; more than that, it was a relief. For a year David had been under terrible conviction of sin and in great misery of heart, as he hid his sin. In Psalm 32 where he tells something of what he went through during that time, he says, ''When I kept silence, my bones waxed old through my groaning all the day long. For day and night thy hand was heavy upon me: my moisture is turned into the drought of summer.''[11] When therefore Nathan came with his challenge, it was welcomed with relief, for it gave him the opportunity to confess and lose his burden. Second, there was immediate confession without any excuses or evasions or self-justification, ''I have sinned against the Lord.''[12] Further, there was also the willingness to be known for what he was in the two psalms of testimony which he wrote.[13] Then, too, he was willing to submit completely to all the discipline God laid upon him, as we have seen.

All of these things showed David, in spite of his tardy confession, to be truly broken before God; and therefore he knew the restoration of the grace of God. And the same can be true of us, although we have to acknowledge that our repentance and confession have been so long delayed.

11. Ps. 32:4. 12. 2 Sam. 12:13. 13. Pss. 32, 51.

11

YOU MUST FORGIVE

Up till now we have had in mind mainly the case of the one who has done the wrong and inflicted the wounds, and his or her need to repent. Now what about the one who has suffered the wrong, sometimes a deep and lasting one? If the offending party must repent, the offended party must forgive. If he does not, he only inflicts further damage on himself. If it is true, "a wounded spirit who can bear?"[1] it is largely because the wounded one will not forgive the other who has inflicted those wounds and carries round with him an unforgiving spirit which eats him up on the inside and only increases his misery. Sometimes a man will not forgive his wife, or a wife her husband, even after there has been confession, and continually makes stabbing reference to what has happened, showing that the root of unforgiveness still remains. Sometimes the unforgiveness has resulted in total rejection of the other and the two have ceased to live together. Often there is bitterness and unforgiveness toward the third party, who has intruded into a marriage and violated it. This sometimes means that a man or woman has a hold over that third party and

1. Prov. 18:14.

indulges the thought that he could ruin him any time he may choose — and may even plan to do so.

Make no mistake, it can be hard and costly truly to forgive another a grievous wrong, for it always means consenting to be thus wronged. We cannot forgive while we are hanging on to our rights and our sense of injury. For instance, if one man forgives another a debt of $1,000, it means he has to consent to suffer that loss himself, to be short by that amount. We cannot forgive without consenting to suffer the loss ourselves.

This is how it is even with God. If He is to forgive a man's sins He has to consent to suffer the loss caused by these sins Himself. He has to consent to be treated as that man has treated Him, if He is to forgive him for doing so. And it was in order that He might actually suffer the loss·and be seen to suffer it that He sent His own Son to die for us on the cross. That is what it cost God to release us.

I remember years ago William Nagenda, one of the leaders in revival in East Africa, speaking on the parable of the Unforgiving Servant. He paused at the point in the parable where the king, moved with compassion toward his bankrupt servant, loosed him and forgave him that immense debt of ten thousand talents of silver. William then went on to imagine what it cost the king to release him. The next day, he imagined, a furniture van was seen at the palace door to take the furniture and all sorts of priceless treasures down to the auction sale. The queen was later seen going out in her old clothes to work as a charwoman in people's homes. Later still, she was seen taking in other people's laundry to raise some more money that way. When the bewildered servant asked what was happening, the king said "It is because I forgave you that debt. It was owing to the exchequer of the realm and it had to be found; so I am paying it myself and this is what it has cost me.'' Just so with the Lord Jesus Christ. So enormous was the debt of human sin that it beggared Him to pay it. ''Though he was rich, yet for your sakes he became poor.''[2] To forgive us He was willing to suffer the enormous loss Himself; there was no other way.

Yes, His forgiveness of us is costly and we shall find that for us to forgive another human is costly too. It means that we must be willing to suffer the loss ourselves if we are going to forgive. We must be willing to be wronged in this or that way, to have our rights trampled on, to be insulted, to be deceived, if we are to forgive the other person doing all this to us. We must be willing to release the other as the king released the servant, but the loss we shall sustain is but a trifle compared to that vast loss that Jesus suffered to forgive us. However, something rises up in us against such a thing; why should *we* have to bear such injustice, why should *we* be treated in this way, it isn't fair, etc. But it is only self that rises up, self that will not lay down its rights and crown at the feet of Jesus. Strange as it may seem, pride lies at the back of that unforgiving spirit, for who are we to say that these things should not happen to us, that our rights should not be trampled on? If God were to deal with us according to our rights, it would be hell for every last one of us sinners. If we are ever to forgive that other, it can be only as we make a deep surrender of self's rights and interests in the matter. And we shall be helped in making that surrender by the knowledge that that was just the surrender He made to forgive us. Why not, then, keep Him company and walk the same path as He?

Be assured, the failure to do this is devastating indeed. Said Jesus, ''If ye do not forgive, neither will your Father

2. 2 Cor. 8:9.

which is in heaven forgive your trespasses.''[3] Don't let
neat theological rationalizations take away from the solemn
warning of those words. They were meant to make a man
who will not forgive, tremble and wonder where he stands.

Where the other party has repented and confessed, it is,
of course, easier to forgive. But deep inside us there may
still be a little root of unforgiveness and we are often
mulling over things in our minds, ''Why did the other do
it? Why did the other deceive me?'' This shows that the
real surrender of self to Jesus on the matter has hardly
taken place. A real surrender must take place, though, if
His cleansing is to reach and heal that wound. And we
shall have to go further; we shall have to accept the thing
that has happened as being allowed by God, as coming from
His hand, to teach everybody in the situation new lessons.
Then we can go on praising Him together, joined in hand
and heart. And a relationship which has been healed by
Him like this is stronger and sweeter than it ever was
before sin came in and damaged it so severely.

The problem cannot but be in some minds — What if the
other does not repent; am I still expected to forgive? The
answer is yes, even as God for Christ's sake offered us
forgiveness long before we ever repented and accepted it.
Of course, God's forgiveness was not made actual until we
repented; it was until then only potential. But the price had
been paid, God had in Christ suffered the loss necessary to
release us and His whole attitude was not that of blaming
sinners and holding their sins over them, but of offering
them His forgiveness. Yes, that was His attitude even
before they had repented, while they were yet sinners,
while they were yet enemies. This is hard to believe, but

3. Mark 11:26.

that this is really His current attitude to sinners is evidenced by the verse "God was in Christ, reconciling the world unto Himself, *not imputing their trespasses unto them*."[4] What can that last phrase mean if not that God is not censuring sinners, but offering them release? Of course, if repentance is refused until the end, then at the great white throne, when the books are opened, God will indeed impute unto men their trespasses and the result will be everlasting banishment from His presence. But until that day God is not imputing unto men their trespasses, because He has already suffered the loss of them Himself in His Son. Nothing melts men to repentance more than having this newly revealed to them by the Holy Spirit.

Now this should be our attitude to those who have wronged us. Our forgiveness is to be completely there for them, though until they repent, reconciliation at this stage is only potential, not actual. And all this is because we have made the essential surrender of self on the matter. Even though they may not have repented as yet, we release them, we "take the heat off them," our personal rights in the matter have been surrendered to God. That leaves God free to work in their hearts toward melting them. But if we still have roots of bitterness and hatred toward them, then our forgiveness of them is not even potential, and our attitude is more likely to make them defend and harden themselves. There is no doubt this is a costly matter and may need more than one visit to the Cross of Jesus before it is settled, but settled it must be.

Yet a further problem may be in some minds. Some may say, the wrong I have sustained is one that is likely to last long, perhaps all my days. How can I be at peace under such long-lasting wrong and injustice? The only answer to

4. 2 Cor. 5:19.

this is what has just been mentioned. It is to accept what has happened as coming from the hand of our loving heavenly Father and submit to it as the yoke He has given us to wear. But you ask, Can it really be that God Himself is in what has happened? I think we can say yes, if we see that each one of us is standing in the center of a circle, a circle which we can call the will of God. Nothing therefore can touch me from outside the circle, unless it has first penetrated that circle. The thing in question may be hurtful, unfair, and callous, but no matter how it originated, by the time it has reached me, it has passed through the circle of the will of God; it has become God's will for me; it has been permitted for wise and good purposes of His own.

> "In the centre of the circle
>   Of the will of God I stand;
> There can be no second causes,
>   All must come from His dear hand."

Therefore in resenting it and refusing it, I am in reality rebelling against God and His will — and I succeed only in making myself more wretched. This is a hard saying; who can hear it? But it is in hearing it, and submitting to that will, that the soul finds peace and reconciliation with God. And reconciliation with God is what we need at this point, for so often we are not reconciled with God and with what He has allowed; indeed we blame Him for it and even hate Him, as we sob in our bitterness.

This is what He meant when He said, "Take my yoke upon you, and learn of me; for I am meek and lowly in heart: and ye shall find rest unto your souls. For my yoke is easy, and my burden is light."[5] The yoke is made for the

5. Matt. 11:29.

neck of a beast. It pictures the will of God, while the neck pictures the will of man. But man's will is stubborn, or as the Scriptures put it, he is stiffnecked[6] and the yoke of the Divine will does not naturally fit across it. If we are to take that yoke, we must be willing to bend our stiff necks, that is, submit. Only so will we find rest to our souls. If we find it hard thus to submit, He lovingly calls it "*My yoke*" — that is, the yoke which He himself wore for us. He was willing to submit Himself to the will of His Father, and the wearing of that yoke led Him in meekness to suffer on the cross for us. He is not asking us to do anything which He has not done for us in an infinitely greater degree. And if it still seems hard to bend our necks to His will, He tells us it is a double yoke, He in one part of the yoke and a place for us in the other part at His side, and He will bear it with us. That surely is why He added the words "and learn of Me, for I am meek and lowly in heart." He is the One who always bowed His head to the Father, was always meek and lowly in heart, and if we are willing to walk with Him, acknowledging to Him how proud and hard we are, we shall learn of the One by our side, and bow our heads as He bowed and still bows His. Our willingness to bow our necks in submission to what He has allowed will move His heart toward us and He will bestow upon us many a sweet evidence of His love for us and many a compensation.

6. Acts 7:51.

12

THE DIVORCE COURT OR THE CROSS?

Divorce is now so easy to obtain and so acceptable socially that it is considered with many to be the obvious way out when a couple does not get along too well. Sometimes at the first hint of trouble, without waiting to see if there is another way round their problem, off the partners march to their respective lawyers and thence to the divorce court. The welfare of the children gives pause for a moment's thought, but often for not much more. Their differences seem to be so irreconcilable that even the children's highest good must be sacrificed to their parents' desire to separate and find new mates. The real cause is not always a big issue between them, but simply the unwillingness of one to give way to the other in a succession of quite trivial matters; and even deeper, the refusal of but one of them to say "I'm sorry," and mean it. For lack of that little word "sorry," innumerable marriages have broken down, infinite misery has been caused and incalculable harm has been done to the children and young people in those families. Divorce always creates more problems than it solves.

What is perhaps the most disturbing feature in all this is the fact that this irresponsibility with regard to the permanence of the marriage vow has spread in measure to professing Christians. The shame done to the name of Christ makes one want to hide one's face and the easy speed with which some couples take steps to separate fills one with wonder at the immaturity and naiveté which makes them think that divorce provides any real solution.

This state of things is all the more sorrowful when near at hand there stands God's ancient way of reconciling man to man and husband to wife, the Cross of our Lord Jesus Christ. Never was there a more efficacious marriage counseling service than that which Jesus provides there. Alas, so few seem to go there, maybe because it is humbling to do so, and the divorce court seems the easier option. And so it is that the Cross has become the forgotten factor in the healing of homes and the restoration of marriages.

Now let it be understood that there is no couple who do not sometimes have differences and a crossing of wills, no matter how loving or dedicated to God they may appear to be. Such things do not surprise or shock the Lord. He simply intends that when such situations arise they should go, not to the divorce court (such a possibility should never even occur to them), but to the Cross of His dear Son, where barriers can so easily be broken down and hearts made one again. He intends that they should come to the Cross, not once in a lifetime, but again and again as occasion may demand. If you know of a couple who are sweetly united in the Lord and who know this secret, and if you ask them of their experience, I am sure they would say, ''This love and unity of ours? It is no thanks to us; left to ourselves we would have drifted apart. It has come from the

Cross of Jesus; it is because there is power in His blood to cleanse sin and restore love.''

The Cross of Jesus, then, is not only the means by which man is reconciled to God, but the means also by which man is reconciled to his fellowman. For if sin causes barriers between man and God, it also causes barriers between man and man and between a man and his wife. And the way by which the Cross reconciles man to man is not very dissimilar to the way it reconciles man to God.

How then does the cross reconcile man to God? For long centuries God sought to humble man and get him to accept the blame of his sin in order that God might then forgive him and restore him to Himself. He brought many and grievous disciplines upon the race to that end, but all to no avail: man would not be broken — he persistently refused to take the blame and return to the Lord. At last it was as if God said, ''If man will not be broken, I will be. If man will not take the blame, I will take the blame.'' That is what happened at the cross; it was God in Christ taking the blame, He the just for us the unjust. This was the divine strategy to bring man back to Himself. And it worked in a way no other way had! For whenever a man is given a real sight of the Cross, of God taking the blame that was his, he is broken, melted, finished, and cries out, ''O my God, that is my place; Thou art not the wrongdoer, I am! Mine the blame, Thine the love!'' And immediately there is reconciliation between them; man surrenders and God forgives. The brokenness of the Deity has provoked the brokenness of the creature!

In much the same way the Cross of the Lord Jesus effects the reconciliation of a man and his fellow — and we are thinking here especially of a man and his wife. However a trouble between them may begin, it is soon reduced to just one factor: who is wrong? The wife points to the husband and says, "You're the one who is wrong!" He points to her and says, "No, you're wrong!" This mutual accusation cannot but produce tension between them and loving communication is lost. Because neither will break, the situation becomes intolerable. The next step could be that one will contemplate seeing a lawyer. We will imagine that at last one of them is given a new sight of the Cross of Jesus; how it happens we may never know, God has so many means He can use. The one who was arguing that he was right sees the wholly and eternally right One taking the position of the wholly wrong one — dying as a criminal among criminals (there was one on either side of Him), as if He were one Himself. Immediately his words falter and he begins to yield.

It is very difficult to maintain that one is right under the shadow of that Cross. We are right, we say, but are we *wholly* right as He was wholly right? Maybe the other person was wrong to begin with, but has not our reaction to his or her wrong been wrong too, dreadfully wrong? The anger, the bitterness, the words, the hatred, have they not been wrong? When we look at it that way we cannot say we are wholly right; far from it. And yet the wholly right One took the position of the wholly wrong one in order to save us from our sins. Why not then take the place of the wrong one too and confess it? And that is exactly what the one who sees the Cross afresh begins to do. This is what we call being broken.

But notice what happens next; that one goes to the other, not to accuse him or her, but rather to accuse himself and to ask the other's forgiveness for his own sins and reactions. The effect of this so often is to melt the other and he or she begins to repent too of what was wrong in his heart. It is not long then before there is a mutual forgiveness, where before there had been mutual accusation, and we have the beautiful sight of two sinners being reconciled together at the foot of the Cross of Jesus. And the love for one another that had long since flown out of the window begins to return, and that in abundant measure. Just as the brokenness of the Deity seen at the cross provokes the brokenness of the creature, so the brokenness of one of those creatures who has been to the Cross provokes the brokenness of the other, who then also comes to the Cross — and there they are made one again.

It may not always work out for you this way — at least, not immediately. This is no gimmick to get the other to repent. God never violates man's free will, and the other can refuse to humble himself. Only the Holy Spirit can melt and persuade him or her to bow the head, but He is more likely to use your brokenness than anything else. You see, you are no longer pointing at the other's sins, only confessing your own, and some of the tension is obviously released. The thing that the other was reacting against is no longer there and that gives God His chance to work in that heart too. So you be the first at the Cross, not waiting for the other! And even if the other does not immediately join you there, you will have the joy of knowing that your sins in the matter have been washed away and you are at peace with God. But again and again we find that the Cross of Jesus does indeed triumph in both hearts — and in the children's hearts too — and great praise is brought to God over another home gloriously restored.

Here let me tell two stories by way of illustration. The first illustrates how needless it is to go to the divorce court when the way to the Cross is open. An active Christian worker I know married a Christian woman who had recently had a divorce from her first husband, who was himself a Christian and had subsequently married again. There is a mess for you — Christians divorcing one another! There is also involved here the rights and wrongs of the remarriage of divorced persons, which question it is not my purpose to go into just now, for the point of my quoting it here is quite other. Strange as it may seem, this active Christian man never inquired deeply into what went wrong with that first marriage until after he had married the lady. As she opened up to him, he began to counsel her on the way of repentance. As a result she was convicted of the wrong of her attitudes and she began to repent. After a time she felt she must write to her former husband, asking his forgiveness. No reply came for some months and when at last one did come it was to tell her that he had seen his wrong too, and would she forgive him! Can you see it — they need never have had that divorce; the shame of it need never have happened, and the complications of a second marriage (and there were complications) could have been avoided, if only they had gone to the Cross; but alas, they went to the divorce court instead.

The second story illustrates positively the glorious triumphs of the Cross in matters like this. I was attending the meeting of a Canadian friend of mine on a visit to Britain in which he was telling of revival in his part of the world. When he finished, he asked if there was anybody who would like to add something in the spirit of the message. A woman, unknown to everybody, walked up to the platform. She told us she was a Canadian visiting Britain, and seeing the announcement of that meeting to be addressed by a Canadian, she decided to come along to hear her fellow-countryman. She told us that though she was a professing Christian, she and her husband had been having a hard time living together and had decided to part. Her son was away at college hardly expecting that there would be any home for him to come back to. The couple had fixed the date when they would sign the papers that would commence divorce proceedings. However, the day before they were due to do this they heard that unusual things were happening in their church under the revival ministry of a visiting preacher. They decided to attend that night and they found themselves confronted by the Lord Jesus Himself, and each saw his sin in His light. Both came to His Cross and were brought into peace with God and to a beautiful reconciliation with one another. A message was sent immediately to the son, ''There is a home for you to come back to after all. We both love the Lord now!'' As if that was not enough, she went on to tell us that the home which had been on the point of breaking up was now filled once a week with some thirty people gathered for a fellowship meeting to share their experiences of the Lord. We listened enrapt to this unrehearsed story of the couple who went to the Cross rather than to the divorce court, with such happy and glorious results. When we contemplate the doings of the Lord like this we may well sing:

> ''O for a thousand tongues to sing
> My great Redeemer's praise!
> The glories of my God and King,
> The triumphs of His grace.''

13

"SIN SHALL NOT HAVE DOMINION OVER YOU"[1]

Be assured, sex in one form or another is everybody's battle, whether male or female, whether non-Christian or true believer. What is one of God's most beautiful gifts to man — and when rightly used, one of the sources of his greatest happiness — has become one of his greatest battlegrounds with evil. Perhaps this is due to the fact that whereas all man's faculties have been affected by the Fall, the sex instinct seems to have become more corrupted by that Fall than any other of his instincts — shown by the fact that the erotic side of our natures responds more readily to evil suggestion than to good. For instance, the story in the newspapers of some illicit sex happening tends to spark off something wrong in us, that the story of another person's happy married life does not. It is undeniable that there is much more public interest in wrong sex than in right sex. And this is our battle even as Christians, no matter how long we have known the Lord. And if we do not know God's way of victory here, we do not know it anywhere. The level of our general Christian lives is not likely to rise any higher than the level of our sex life.

1. Rom. 6:14.

Even when the Christian is free from outward practices, the battle is on with regard to unclean thoughts, unclean desires, and unclean private practices. And also, alas, he is not always victorious here, pray as he will. This fact is extremely dangerous and that from two points of view. If he cannot as a Christian ''get the victory'' (as the saying goes) he may be tempted to say, ''What is the use of being a Christian at all?'' and giving up his profession altogether, go back into the world. Perhaps that is the rationale behind some cases of backsliding — not that the world is so attractive, but that the person concerned cannot ''make the Christian life work'' and so gives up. On the other hand, he may settle for something less than the best and rationalize these things. He may say, for instance, that self-abuse (masturbation) is normal, everybody does it, even Christians, and he ceases to call it sin. If what he says is really true (everybody does it, even Christians), we need not look any further for the reason for the lack of revival in our churches: everybody is play-acting, everybody is hiding sin.

But under grace there is no need for either of these alternatives. There is no need either to despair and give up, or to hide sin and play the hypocrite. I say ''under grace,'' for the great text at the head of this chapter, ''sin shall not have dominion over you,'' is followed by the words ''for ye are not under the law, but under grace.''[2] If we are to experience sin not having dominion over us, we shall have to know truly what it is to be living under grace and not under law.

But first of all we must understand what sin not having dominion over us really means. Part of our trouble stems from having a wrong conception of what this is. This was

2. Rom. 6:14.

certainly true in my own case. I used to think it was promised that I could get to a place where I would have no more problem with sin, that I would be dead to its solicitations. But I never could assert that I had got to that place and I came to hate this text and the chorus based on it which I had to sing at the Bible class I attended:

> "Sin shall not have dominion over you;
> Oh what a glorious message and it's true."

I hated it because it did not seem to work in my experience, not only in the matter of sex, but over my Christian life generally. As I have said, part of my trouble was that I did not understand truly what was wrong, and that in turn was based on a wrong conception of what the dominion of sin over me really consisted of. Latterly I have come to see that the dominion of sin is not firstly its ability to fascinate me, to entice me to yield and through constant repetition on my part to form itself into a habit, but rather that its dominion consists in the guilt which it always leaves behind as its legacy. By guilt I do not mean something merely objective standing against us in the books of God, but something subjective and internal, a hangover of shame and accusation which is always left behind after the committing of sin, whatever its particular character may be. The passage of time does nothing to obliterate that guilt, just as leaving for days or weeks a cup from which one has drunk coffee does nothing to remove the stains within it. This invests sin with a far greater power than we thought; i.e., its power to condemn us and to go on condemning us long after we have committed it. In such a case the most we can hope to do is to keep the cupboard door firmly closed on the skeleton; but the deep inner malaise continues, only to be increased by the committing of further sins. This is what it really means to be under the dominion of sin.

I know we Christians have been taught to believe that the guilt of sin is one thing, and the power of sin another, if only through the hymns we sing. Toplady's great hymn, "Rock of Ages," has the words "Save me from sin's guilt and power." It is generally understood that the guilt of sin was blotted out when we first accepted Jesus Christ as our Saviour, but to be set free from its daily power to seduce is another thing altogether. And it is thought another blessing, some second blessing, is needed to attain that end. This certainly used to be my own understanding; but I have come to see that the guilt and power of sin are not two separate things, but that the power of sin over me consists in its guilt, its power to condemn me. This means that it is possible for a man to have committed a certain sin years ago, a sin which he has never committed since, and yet to be under its dominion to this day, if only because it is still condemning him. Its hang-over of guilt is still there in his heart, either consciously or subconsciously. In that condition his relationship with God is of course blurred, and he lacks the peace and joy that is promised to believers. More than that, his relationship with his fellows is affected and he becomes withdrawn and unable to communicate, because there is so much he dare not be open about.

In such a condition of spiritual deadness, the natural thing for all of us is to turn to what Paul calls in this verse, "The law." By this I mean we espouse higher standards for ourselves and try to do better; we determine to be more spiritual and hope to apply ourselves to our religious duties more conscientiously, and we do all this in the hope that it will bring about the much-needed change in our relationship with God and our fellows. But it does no such thing, and that because, excellent as these new goals may be, we never quite succeed in attaining them or in becoming more spiritual people. And our failure to do so only adds to our sense of condemnation and makes our situation worse, not better. This is what Paul means when he says elsewhere, "the strength of sin is the law."[3] You would think that he would have said "the strength of sin is temptation, but the strength of holiness is the law." But no — the strength of sin is the law, because those unattained ideals of the law of God only give sin more about which to condemn us. Had we not so hopefully espoused those higher standards we would not feel so condemned. If the dominion of sin over us is its power to condemn us, then the holy law of God only adds to that power.

In that condition of despair we have little motivation but to commit futher sin. Our spiritual situation is so dead and unsatisfying that we feel a further act of sin is not going to make things much worse — so why not? When on Sunday morning a clean tablecloth is put on the table everybody in the family is very careful not to upset things on it; but halfway through the week there are so many stains on it that nobody cares if he makes another stain — it is all part of the general pattern. The most we can hope for in this situation is to try to hide some of the more shameful stains. But the longer we hide sin, the longer it goes on condemning us and we get more and more under its dominion.

Is it not obvious from all this that the real purpose of Satan in provoking us to commit sin is not merely that we might do something unethical, but that when we have done it, he might have the opportunity to accuse us (he is called the accuser of the brethren in Revelation 12), and then in that condition we are rendered powerless in our Christian

3. 1 Cor. 15:56.

witness and service. The Christian who has committed an impure act feels himself the next day an utter dog; he does not want to look God or his fellow-Christians in the eye; and as for undertaking some spiritual service — he would rather run away and hide. This is just the result the devil intended when he provoked that Christian to sin. He hopes that this will lead to further sin and that in turn will give him the opportunity to accuse him further and so on and so on. The sin is one thing, but the superstructure of guilt the devil builds on it is another, and is sometimes far greater than the original sin on which it is built.

To understand, then, the true nature of the dominion of sin and what are the devil's intentions in it is the first step into freedom.

We are now ready to hear the message of grace. The grace of God is the love of God in action toward those who deserve nothing and can do nothing. The law has certainly reduced us to that place, and in doing so has actually made us candidates for grace. The supreme thing that the grace of God has done for such people is to provide for them a Saviour. As the chorus puts it,

> "When none was found to deliver me,
> Jesus came, praise His Name!"

Or better, as the Apostle John says, "Herein is love, not that we loved God, but that he loved us, and sent his Son to be the propitiation for our sins."[4] Calvary shows us we are loved by God as we are, unconditionally, without strings. There Jesus died not only *for* sin, but *to* sin. That is how Romans 6 puts it: "In that he died, he died *unto* sin once."[5] What does that mean? It does not mean that He

4. 1 John 4:10.   5. Rom. 6:10.

died to sin's solicitations (He was never alive to them); but that in paying our debt in His blood He died to sin's power to condemn Him any longer and therefore God raised Him from the dead. But if at that cross sin lost its power to condemn our Substitute, it has also lost its power to condemn all those whose Substitute He became. If each one of them now returns to the Cross in confession, they may all reckon on this fact, lose their burden of guilt, and step into freedom. Whereas the law demands that we do our utmost (with no result but further condemnation, as we have seen), grace points to Christ as having done all for us and bids us reckon ourselves dead with Him to the power of our sins to condemn us any longer.

In some ears the expression "return to the Cross" may seem just a religious cliché, without much meaning save for the initiated. When it comes to experience, I can assure you it is no cliché, but a very deep and humbling thing. It means returning to the place before God of a self-confessed sinner, and to the place where pardon and restoration are freely offered. If we take a long time to do that, we will be a long time under the dominion of sin. But the moment we humble ourselves and confess it all, we are forgiven, cleansed, set free from guilt and declared right with God — and all because of the age-abiding value in the eyes of God of the blood of Jesus. The foundation of guilt on which Satan built his superstructure is removed by God Himself; the superstructure itself comes tumbling down and the one imprisoned within it is set free.

This is the sense in which we are to interpret this great word of promise, "sin shall not have dominion over you." It is also the sense in which we are to interpret other important phrases in Romans 6: "being made free from sin,"[6] and "we, that are dead to sin";[7] free from and dead to

6. Rom. 6:18, 22.   7. v. 2.

sin, not in the sense of being free or dead to its solicitations, but to its power to condemn us — and therefore free from all the baneful consequences of being under its guilt, which we have already indicated.

Then further, under grace a new motivation comes to the liberated soul, the motivation of love. He that is forgiven much loves much.[8] Under law there was just no other motivation than fear, the fear of sin and the fear of guilt which nothing he could do would remove. But under grace, under the shadow of the Cross of Jesus, the guilt is gone, the accusations of Satan are silenced, the conscience is made whiter than snow, and a mighty new motivation comes into our hearts, the motivation of love for the One who has done all this for us. This motivation leads us to quit the sin and to present ourselves and our members as slaves to the One who has done it all. And with that motivation come blessed reinforcements of the will from the Holy Spirit who now dwells within us. And the result is holiness, real practical holiness right here and now, and the end everlasting life. Indeed, that is precisely how Romans 6 sums it all up: "But now being made free from sin, and become slaves to God, ye have your fruit unto holiness, and the end everlasting life."[9]

So it is that under grace there is no need to despair because of sin, when in some form it is again part of our experience. The blood of Jesus is ever available for our restoration and cleansing. In this new situation sin still need not have dominion over us for any longer than it takes us to get to the Cross again and confess it. Nor, on the other hand, need we feel that we can only cover up our failures and thus play the hypocrite. Under grace we can afford to be honest and call sin, sin, without any excuse.

8. See Luke 8:36-50.　　　　9. Rom. 6:22.

Indeed, we must do so if the Father is to run and embrace us, even as the father did in the parable of his returning son. And nothing will encourage us to do this so much as a new sight of God as the God of grace, the sinner's God. Thereafter our testimony to others is not that of the Pharisee — "I have not been like other men"; but that of the Publican — "God has been merciful to me, a sinner."[10]

But be careful about using this word "again" with regard to a sin you have committed, lest you miss the power of the blood of Jesus. If you say "Lord, I've done it again," I know what He will say: "What have you done again?" With Him there is no record of its ever having happened before — such is the power of His blood. If you know what it is to go the Cross, there is no need to load yourself with what has gone before; as far as He is concerned this is the first time you have ever come to Him with that thing. Thus it is that after every new coming to Jesus, you may say with joy, "This day is the first day of the rest of my life."

10. See Luke 18:10-14.